D1630522

Edexcel AS Music
Revision Guide

by

Alistair Wightman

R· RHINEGOLD
EDUCATION

www.rhinegoldeducation.co.uk

First published 2013 in Great Britain by
Rhinegold Education
14–15 Berners Street
London W1T 3LJ
www.rhinegoldeducation.co.uk

© 2013 Rhinegold Education
a division of Music Sales Limited

You should always check the current requirements of the examination, since these may change. Copies of the Edexcel specification may be downloaded from the Edexcel website at www.edexcel.com. Telephone: 01623 467467, Fax: 01623 450481, Email: publications.orders@edexcel.com.

Edexcel AS Music Revision Guide
British Library Cataloguing in Publication Data.
A catalogue record for this book is available from the British Library.
Order No. RHG335
ISBN 978-1-78305-032-1

Exclusive Distributors:
Music Sales Ltd
Distribution Centre, Newmarket Road
Bury St Edmunds, Suffolk IP33 3YB, UK

Printed in the EU

Contents

THE AUTHOR

Alistair Wightman read Music at Oxford and then York University, where he was awarded a D. Phil for his study of the music of Karol Szymanowski. He has worked in primary, secondary and further education, and is a freelance teacher and writer as well as principal examiner in history and analysis in A-level music. His publications include *Writing About Music* (Rhinegold, 2008) and several books and articles devoted to Tadeusz Baird, Karłowicz and Szymanowski, including *Karłowicz, Young Poland and the Musical Fin-de-siècle* (Ashgate, 1996), *Karol Szymanowski: his Life and Music* (Ashgate, 1999) and *Szymanowski on Music: Selected Writings of Karol Szymanowski* (Toccata Press, 1999).

COPYRIGHT

Introduction

For the AS qualification in music you have to complete the following units:
* Unit 1: Performing Music (30% of the total AS mark)
* Unit 2: Composing (30% of the total AS mark)
* Unit 3: Developing Musical Understanding (40% of the total AS mark).

This guide will help you to revise for Unit 3, an externally assessed examination which lasts for two hours. In particular, we deal here with Section B (Investigating Musical Styles) – the written part of the exam that requires you to answer two questions about various musical features of the set works.

Pages 9–13 contain an overview of the **terminology** that will be used in the Section B questions, along with a list of the type of **features** you would be expected to mention in your answers.

This is followed by **revision notes** on each of the set works for your exam year, and a series of **sample essay questions and answers** for Section B. The revision notes provide a succinct overview of the most important technical features of the music: rhythm and metre, melody, harmony, tonality, structure, texture and performance resources. The sample essay questions will help you to put your knowledge into practice, and learn how to write answers that will achieve the highest marks.

For practice materials for Sections A and C, consult Rhinegold Education's *Edexcel AS Music Listening Tests, 4th edition* (2013).

The marks for Unit 3 are distributed as follows:
* Section A (Listening) is worth 40% of the paper total
* Section B (Investigating Musical Styles) is worth 35% of the paper total
* Section C (Understanding Chords and Lines) is worth 25% of the paper total.

At the start of the summer term, it is quite likely that you will still be finishing Units 1 and 2. It is in your interests to complete these assignments as soon as you can in order to maximise the time available for preparing for the Unit 3 examination.

SET WORKS

Sections A and B in the exam are closely linked in that they both focus on the set works that you will have studied as part of your AS-level course. The set works change every year, so you need to make sure you are studying the correct ones for the year you are taking the examination. The set works for 2014 and 2015 are as follows:

Instrumental music 2014

- Haydn – Symphony No. 26 in D minor, 'Lamentatione': movement I
- Holborne – Pavane 'The image of melancholy' and Galliard 'Ecce quam bonum'
- Brahms – Piano Quintet in F minor, Op. 34: movement III
- Debussy – Pour le piano: Sarabande

Vocal music 2014

- Stravinsky – Symphony of Psalms: movement III
- Weelkes – Sing we at pleasure
- Schubert – Der Doppelgänger
- Howlin' Wolf – I'm leavin' you
- Desmond Dekker and the Aces – You can get it if you really want

Instrumental music 2015

- Bach – Brandenburg Concerto No. 4 in G: movement I
- Shostakovich – String Quartet No. 8, Op. 110: movement I
- Poulenc – Sonata for Horn, Trumpet and Trombone: movement I
- Mozart – Piano Sonata in B♭, K. 333: movement I

Vocal music 2015

- Tavener – The Lamb
- Monteverdi – Ohimè, se tanto amate
- Fauré – Après un rêve
- The Kinks – Waterloo Sunset
- Van Morrison – Tupelo Honey
- Familia Valera Miranda (Cuba) – Se quema la chumbambá

In Section A of the exam, there are two questions: the first will draw on one of the instrumental set works, and the second on one of the vocal set works. You have to answer both of them.

For Section B of the exam, you can choose to answer questions on either the instrumental or vocal set works.

So even if you decide before the exam that, for Section B, you are only going to answer questions on the vocal set works, you still need to revise the instrumental set works as well in order to cope with the demands of Section A. (Revision notes for the 2014 set works can be found on pages 14–29, and for the 2015 set works on pages 60–75.)

SECTION A: LISTENING

As stated above, there are two questions in Section A. In the exam, for each question, you will be played a short extract from one of the set works (which you will hear five times). You will also be provided with a skeleton score of the extract, showing locations of most of the features you have to describe.

You will have to demonstrate your analytical knowledge and aural skills by identifying aspects such as:

- Instruments and/or voices
- Textures
- Rhythmic devices and patterns
- Melodic aspects
- Features of word setting
- Keys, cadences and chords
- Harmonic devices
- Structure of the extract
- The location of the extract within the set work.

As the questions in Section A are based on the set works, by the time you get to the exam you should already be very familiar with the music you will hear, and to a great extent you will be able to rely on information you have already memorised to answer the questions.

While you are practising listening questions as part of your revision, make sure you form the habit of:

- Seeing how many marks are available for each question (and therefore how many points you are expected to make)
- Working out plausible possibilities (such as related keys) to support your answers
- Using correct terms (keep referring back to the terminology section on pages 9–13 of this book).

This revision guide is primarily focused on Section B of the exam, but there is lots of help and practice questions for Section A in *Edexcel AS Music Listening Tests*, 4th *edition* (Rhinegold Education, 2013).

SECTION B: INVESTIGATING MUSICAL STYLES

The rest of this book is focused on Section B of the exam, which requires you to answer two written questions on the set works. This book will help you to:

- Revise the key facts for each set work
- Practise writing essay answers that incorporate those key facts
- Improve the way you express your ideas, helping you to gain higher marks.

Remember that in this section of the exam, you are going to focus on just one of the areas of study, either instrumental or vocal music. Whichever area you select, you will have to answer two questions:

- The first, marked out of 10, will focus on stylistic and historical aspects
- The second, marked out of 18, will involve comparing and contrasting specific features of two of the set works.

In the exam you should allow yourself approximately one hour for this section, perhaps allotting up to 20 minutes for the first question and up to 35 minutes for the second.

Here are a few tips to remember for the exam:

- Use the correct musical terms wherever possible (for example, describe the texture as 'monophonic' rather than 'thin').
- Remember to make sure that *everything* you write is in some way answering the question (if a question asks you to write about 'rhythm' and 'melody', for example, you won't get any marks for writing about harmony!).
- You don't necessarily need to write out any music examples in order to get full marks; and because you can't take a copy of the Anthology into the exam, you won't be expected to mention specific bar numbers either. (Having said that, do try to be as precise as possible when talking about specific sections of the music.)

Be aware that you will be marked in this part of the exam on Quality of Written Communication (QWC), which means that the examiners will evaluate the quality of your writing. This will involve aspects such as:

- Organisation, planning and coherence
- Grammar and spelling
- The appropriate use of terminology.

This doesn't mean that you have to write an answer in continuous prose; it is perfectly possible to answer in note form, but you should still be careful to express yourself as clearly as possible, grouping your ideas together in a logical, coherent sequence.

Although this section of the exam might seem daunting, the type of questions you will be asked are actually very predictable. This means that if you revise carefully, and do enough practice questions, it is perfectly feasible to earn full marks. The rest of this book will help you to get closer to this goal.

Terminology

This section includes many of the terms you will need to know for your exam, but it is not exhaustive. It may well also be the case that you will not need to comment on all the points listed below for each and every set work. Having said that, this section will certainly give you a good idea of the sort of things you should be writing about when, for example, you are asked to comment on 'melody' or 'texture' in the exam.

RHYTHM AND METRE

When writing about rhythm and metre, think about commenting on:

- The variety of note lengths
- Recurring rhythmic patterns
- Dotted rhythms
- Syncopation
- Hemiola
- Triplets or other tuplets
- The time signature – whether it is simple or compound, duple, triple, quadruple or quintuple
- Metre changes
- Whether there is a metre at all.

MELODY

When writing about melody, think about commenting on:

- The range of the melody
- Whether it is in a major or minor key, or else modal or atonal
- Whether it is diatonic or chromatic
- The phrase structure – whether it is made up of balanced phrases ('periodic' phrasing) or something less regular
- Use of repetition or sequence
- Whether the melody is on a monotone (single pitch), conjunct (moving by step) or disjunct (moving by leap). If moving by leap, be ready to describe some of the intervals
- Particular stylistic characteristics – for example in early music, the tendency to follow a leap with a step
- Use of motifs
- Whether the melody line is flowing or broken up by rests.

If you are describing vocal music, you could also comment on aspects of word setting:

- Whether the setting is syllabic (one note per syllable) or melismatic (several notes to a syllable)
- Whether verbal and musical accents coincide – in other words, whether the stressed syllables fall on the first beat or other strong beats of the bar, or not.

HARMONY

Here you should comment on the music's vertical structure – the chords – and how they proceed from one to another. You may have to consider whether the chord is:

- A primary or secondary triad
- An augmented or diminished triad
- In root position or inverted
- Diatonic or chromatic
- Functional (broadly speaking, when the chord progressions help to define the key), or whether unrelated chords are used.

Other harmonic devices you may have to describe include:

- Cadences (perfect, imperfect/Phrygian, plagal, interrupted)
- Tonic or dominant pedals (specify which)
- Circle of 5ths
- Tierce de Picardie.

You should also be prepared to comment on the presence of particular types of dissonance:

- Suspension
- False relation
- Appoggiatura
- 7th chords, or one of the higher dissonances (9th, 11th, 13th) – and also whether they are resolved
- Added 6th, augmented 6th, diminished 7th, Neapolitan 6th
- Added-note chords.

TONALITY

Tonality is not another word for sound quality or timbre. It is about whether the music has a key, and you should be ready to consider the following points:

- Is the music tonal or atonal?
- If the music is tonal, is the harmony functional (with cadences defining the key)?
- Is the harmony non-functional? Perhaps the music still has a key signature, but is better regarded as being 'on' rather than 'in' the key.
- Some pieces might be modal – in which case, name the mode and the key it is based on. (Be careful: the music may not be modal throughout, or else may change modes as it goes on.)
- Does the music modulate (change key systematically over a number of bars), as in most classical works, or does it abruptly shift from one tonal centre to another?

> Remember that in tonality questions, marks will be available for associating a theme with its key, such as observing that the second subject of Haydn's Symphony No. 26 (movement I) is in F major. Bar numbers would not be expected by the examiner because you do not have access to the Anthology in the exam.

TEXTURE

This term applies to the way parts are combined to sound together, and also the number of parts involved. The number of parts will affect the density of the sound. Types of texture include:

> **Special warning:** it is not enough at this level to describe a texture as 'thick' or 'thin'. You should aim, wherever possible, to state the number of parts, as well as the type of texture involved.

Monophonic	A single (unaccompanied) melody.
Polyphonic	This term tends to be used as another way of saying contrapuntal – the combination of independently moving melody lines. It is generally better to reserve its use for early music, especially choral music of the Renaissance era.
Contrapuntal	See above. This term is freely applied in discussions of music from any period. The combination of independently moving lines may be: • Free: when there is no melodic similarity between the parts • Imitative: when another part enters with the same theme while the first continues with its own music • Canonic: a strict form of imitation, when the second part is near enough an exact copy of the first, even if at a different pitch • Fugal: as in a fugue or fugato.
Homophony	Chordal textures, sometimes also described as 'homorhythmic': all parts having the same rhythm. Melody-dominated homophony: textures in which the melody is supported by a rhythmically independent part – for example, Alberti bass or broken-chord patterns. You may prefer to use the expression 'melody and accompaniment'. > In movements which are rarely anything other than homophonic, don't forget to mention transfers of the melody from treble to bass, changes in accompanying patterns, and the numbers of parts (the density) used at any one time.
Heterophony	When a melody line is heard along with a rhythmically different or melodically varied version of itself.
Antiphony	When passages of music are performed by different singers and/or instrumentalists in alternation. The groups do not have to be evenly balanced. 'Call and response' also refers to antiphony, particularly in jazz and popular music.

Other textural features include:

- Octaves – don't forget to say how many octaves there are, or to differentiate between octaves and unison.
- Pedal notes – also regarded as harmonic and tonal devices, although they have some bearing on the make-up of texture as well.
- Ostinato – a short repeated melodic and/or rhythmic figure, heard in conjunction with other musical ideas. It also plays a prominent role in the overall texture.
- Riff – a term for ostinato used in connection with jazz and popular music.

PERFORMANCE FORCES AND TIMBRE

'Performance forces' simply means the voices and instruments used.

'Timbre' refers to the nature of the sounds being produced. Think about commenting on the use of particular ranges, where this has an effect on the overall sound being created. For example, when generally low sounds are used to produce a melancholic mood.

Also be ready to describe the effects of unusual playing techniques, such as the use of mutes, harmonics or different bowing techniques.

If asked to compare and contrast the performance forces of particular pieces, it may not be enough just to list the names of the instruments involved. You will need to show that you understand the essential differences between the works by commenting further, perhaps referring to historical periods and issues of authenticity, or else the role played by the instruments in the texture.

STRUCTURE

Many questions will require you to comment on the structure or form of a given work.

The structures that you need to know for the 2014 and 2015 set works are:

Having identified the structure, avoid falling back on an abstract or vague description of the music. This tends to be a particular temptation in sonata form movements.

2014	2015
Binary	Ternary
Ternary	Ritornello form
Rondo	Sonata form
Scherzo and trio	Strophic
Sonata form	Through-composed
Strophic	Verse and chorus
Through-composed	
Twelve-bar blues	
Verse and chorus	

Once you have identified the structure in general terms, be ready to give a more detailed description of the main sections in the music, giving changes of key and specific descriptive terms (e.g. first subject, exposition, and so on).

CIRCUMSTANCES OF PERFORMANCE

Questions are frequently asked in the exam about the location of the original performance, the nature of the audience and perhaps the purpose of the music. In the course of your revision, try to establish the date and place of the first performance wherever possible. Sometimes this will not be possible, especially in the case of earlier music, and in these cases make sure that you have a plausible general idea (for example, Holborne's Pavane and Galliard were evidently designed for domestic use, drawing on any available instruments). In the case of sacred vocal music, it would not normally be enough to say 'in a church'.

When writing about sacred music, be ready to comment on whether the music is actually appropriate for church performance (Stravinsky's *Symphony of Psalms* was for concert use), and if so, the type of church and the place of the particular piece of music in the service or liturgy.

When writing about jazz or popular music, you may need to differentiate between live performance and studio recording.

Revision notes 2014

Here we have provided a series of revision notes that will help you to focus on the most important aspects of each set work. It would not be wise to try to memorise everything for a parrot-like recitation of facts and figures. We suggest instead that you check you understand the main points, or generalisations, given under the various headings. After this, try to absorb some of the additional examples, which will often then help you to think of your own examples that can be used to illustrate the work in question.

It is most important that you keep referring to the Edexcel Anthology, and associate the points made in the following pages with what you hear in the music and see in the score. Any attempt to learn these points in the form of abstract crib notes means you do not get anything out of the exercise in the long term, and run the risk of error in the exam.

INSTRUMENTAL MUSIC 2014

Haydn – Symphony No. 26 in D minor, 'Lamentatione': movement I

Background	• Haydn was an Austrian composer who wrote more than 100 symphonies, and was important in establishing the genre as the most significant type of orchestral music in the Classical period.
	• This excerpt is the first movement of a three-movement symphony.
	• It was probably composed in 1768, to be played in a concert hall by the small professional court orchestra of the Hungarian Prince Esterházy, for whom Haydn was music director.
	• The nickname 'Lamentatione' ('Lamentation') refers to the inclusion of a plainsong melody associated with the suffering and death of Jesus Christ, reflecting the intention that the work would be performed in the week before Easter.
	• The movement reflects the *Sturm und Drang* ('Storm and Stress') style of the early Classical period, with its minor-key opening, agitated syncopation, tense harmonies and vivid contrasts.
Rhythm and metre	• The time signature of **C** is a simple quadruple metre (four crotchet beats in a bar) and the tempo is fairly fast.
	• Most bars feature quaver movement, sometimes provided by syncopated crotchets in the upper parts against on-beat crotchets in the bass (such as at the start of the movement). The countermelody to the second subject consists of almost continuous quavers.
	• Wind instruments sometimes have more sustained parts.
	• Syncopation creates a sense of urgency in the opening passage and similar sections.
	• Short rests (e.g. at the ends of bars 8 and 16) clarify the ends of sections.

Melody	• The opening (the first subject) has two melodic strands: the syncopated upper part and the 'walking bass', heard together in counterpoint. Both feature stepwise movement and mainly small leaps.
	• The second main melodic idea (the second subject) is the plainsong cantus firmus introduced by oboe and second violins in bar 17. Like most plainsong, it includes repeated notes and mainly conjunct movement, with only a few small leaps, while the first-violin countermelody above it is based largely on broken chords.
	• Both melodies are diatonic – the first in D minor and the second in the relative major (F major).
	• The melody includes ornamentation such as trills and appoggiaturas.
Harmony	• The harmony is functional, with perfect cadences to define keys and mark the ends of sections.
	• Chords I and $V^{(7)}$ also have an important role elsewhere, e.g. to accompany the opening bars of the second subject.
	• Diminished 7th chords, such as in bar 13, generate harmonic tension.
	• Dissonances created by suspensions and long appoggiaturas (e.g. E against D in bar 16) add to the harmonic tension.
	• Harmonic sequences and a circle of 5ths progression occur in the middle section.
Tonality	• The movement is in D minor (although ends in the tonic major, D major).
	• The second subject is in the relative major (F) where it first appears. There are a few modal inflections in the second subject, perhaps because of its plainsong nature.
	• The middle section continues in F major and then passes through various keys on the way to A minor (the dominant minor).
	• The final section returns to D minor, but this time the second subject is in the tonic major (D major).
Structure	• The movement is in sonata form (the most common structure for longer movements in the Classical period).
	• The first section (the exposition) ends at the repeat mark, and consists of the first subject in D minor followed by the second subject in F major.
	• The first 16 bars (and similar passages) use periodic phrasing (balanced phrases in multiples of two and four bars) – one of the most characteristic features of the Classical style.
	• In the middle section (the development), Haydn manipulates material from the first section, passing through a wider range of keys.
	• The final section (the recapitulation) begins with the return of the first subject in D minor. It is followed by the second subject (now in D major) and ends with a brief coda in D major.

Resources	• This work uses a small orchestra of two oboes, bassoon, two horns and strings, typical of the early Classical period.
	• First and second violins play in unison in some passages (such as the start of the movement), while violas often double the cellos (either in unison or an octave higher).
	• The cello part would also have been played by a double bass, sounding an octave below the cellos.
	• The word 'cembalo' at the start of the bass part indicates that a harpsichordist may have filled out the texture by improvising chords based on the cello part.
	• Oboes mainly double the violins, sometimes having a simplified version of their parts.
	• The bassoon doubles the cello part, although drops out in any passages where the oboes don't play.
	• Horns in D sound a minor 7th lower than written. These were 'natural' horns (without valves) and so could play only a limited selection of pitches. They are used mainly in the D-minor and D-major sections.
	• The orchestral parts use a fairly modest range and none are technically very demanding.
Texture	• The orchestral doublings mentioned above result in a texture of just two-part counterpoint in the first eight bars (and similar sections).
	• This is followed by four bars of chordal (or homorhythmic) texture. The contrast is underlined by an abrupt change of dynamic from f to p, and back to f for the start of the second subject. (These abrupt changes in level are known as terraced dynamics.)
	• Elsewhere, and particularly in the plainsong sections, the texture is mainly melody-dominated homophony.
	• The effect of the second violins and oboes doubling the first violins with a simplified version of the same melody creates passages of heterophonic texture.

Holborne – Pavane 'The image of melancholy' and Galliard 'Ecce quam bonum'

Background	• These pieces, first published in 1599, are examples of Elizabethan instrumental music.
	• The pavane and galliard were two of the most popular courtly dances of the time, and were often paired in collections of instrumental music.
	• The music was intended for amateur performance at home and not to accompany dancing.

Rhythm and metre	• Rhythm and metre are the most important elements in distinguishing different styles of dance. Performers would have known the speed at which to play each dance, despite the absence of tempo directions.
	• The Pavane is in fairly slow duple metre, with a variety of note lengths (including a pedal note that lasts for six bars).
	• The Galliard is in lively triple metre, starting with dotted rhythms and featuring the occasional hemiola (e.g. bar 7).
	• Very few rests are used in either dance.
Melody	• All parts have a fairly narrow range.
	• Movement is mainly conjunct: the few large leaps are usually followed by compensating stepwise movement in the opposite direction.
Harmony	• The basic harmony is confined to root-position and first-inversion chords.
	• These are decorated with passing notes and other devices. Features typical of the style include:
	• The many suspensions and occasional false relations in the Pavane.
	• A tierce de Picardie at the end of the first and last sections of the Galliard.
	• A Phrygian cadence to end the middle section of the Galliard.
	• The middle section of the Pavane begins with a six-bar tonic pedal on D.
Tonality	• The Pavane is in D major and the Galliard is in D minor.
	• The harmony is not functional, but cadences and modulations to related keys are still used.
	• Traces of the old modal system persist in features such as the false relations.
Structure	• Both dances have three different sections, each of which is repeated (i.e. AABBCC).
	• Performers would often ornament their part on the repeats.
Resources	• The dances were published as being suitable for bowed strings (viols or violins) and/or wind instruments.
	• In practice, a set of similar instruments of different sizes was preferred, such as a consort of viols or recorders (leading to little variation in timbre).
	• The music was derived from vocal styles and thus is unidiomatic (it was not written with any particular instrument in mind).

Texture	• Both dances have a five-part texture.
	• All parts are of roughly equal importance, although the bass is less active than the other parts.
	• The textures are mainly contrapuntal. Imitation and inversion are used in both dances, such as at the start of the Galliard:
	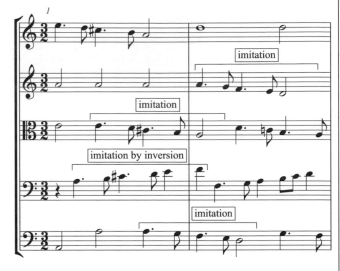
	• The middle section of the Galliard has a more homophonic texture.

Brahms – Piano Quintet in F minor, Op. 34: movement III

Background	• This excerpt is the third movement of a four-movement work, written for piano quintet.
	• A piano quintet is a chamber-music group of five players (a pianist and four string players).
	• The work was completed in 1865 by the German composer Brahms.
	• This movement is a scherzo and trio (a fast triple-time movement consisting of two parts – the 'scherzo' and the 'trio' – although the scherzo is repeated after the trio to create a ternary form).
	• The scherzo and trio evolved out of the earlier minuet and trio, and during the 19th century was a popular form for the third movement of a work.
	• The work is intended for highly skilled (virtuoso) performers and is typically played in small concert halls.

Rhythm and metre	• The movement is mainly in compound duple metre ($\frac{6}{8}$) but with some sections in simple metre ($\frac{2}{4}$).
	• Rhythmic features include:
	• Syncopation (e.g. the opening violin theme)
	• Augmentation
	• Dotted rhythms
	• Cross rhythms in the central section of the trio.
Melody	• Melodies are built from a limited number of motifs. There are three main themes in the scherzo:
	• A: the rising arpeggiated line at the start (which features a rising sequence).
	• B: a theme with repeated staccato notes (first heard at bar 13).
	• C: a march-like melody that is augmented from a small motif in the second theme:
	• These themes are sometimes fragmented, such as in bars 93–100 (where the melody is based on just three notes from theme B).
	• Melodies in the trio are more lyrical and based on rising and falling 3rds.
Harmony	• There is frequent use of chromatic harmony, including:
	• Augmented 6th chords
	• Diminished 7th chords
	• Half-diminished 7th chords
	• Secondary 7ths (such as V^{7}b of VI).
	• There is a preference for imperfect cadences, to keep the music moving forwards. A few different sections end with Phyrgian cadences.
	• Pedal notes are sometimes used (e.g. tonic at the start, dominant in the central section of the trio).
	• There is a circle of 5ths in the trio.

Tonality	• The movement is in C minor, and ends with a tierce de Picardie on a chord of C major. (The central section, the trio, is also in C major.) • Of the three themes mentioned above, A and B first appear in a minor key while C is initially major. • The music modulates frequently, both to related keys (such as the dominant and relative major) and to very distant keys (such as E♭ minor).
Structure	• The scherzo consists of three themes which are heard in the following order: A B C | A A B – fugato – B C | A B • Each theme is modified and developed when it returns. • The long central fugato is based on theme B. • The trio is in ternary form and, because the scherzo is repeated after the trio, the entire movement also forms a ternary structure (scherzo – trio – scherzo).
Resources	• The work is written for two violins, viola, cello and piano. • All parts are very demanding and use a wide range (with high tessituras particularly in the string parts). • The piano part includes dense chords, and single and double octaves. • The string parts include pizzicato and occasional double-stopping. • Brahms' writing is very idiomatic.

Texture	• The wide range of textures includes:
	
	    • Strings in octaves over a tonic pedal at the start of theme A.
	
	    • Free imitation when the piano joins in.
	
	    • Two string instruments in octaves at the start of theme B.
	
	    • A chordal (homorhythmic) texture at the start of theme C.
	
	    • All strings in octaves with the piano in chordal imitation following this.
	
	    • A contrapuntal texture in the fugato (with five independent parts), culminating in a stretto in which entries of the theme come closer together.
	
	    • Piano homophony with a cello pedal at the start of the trio, followed by homophonic strings with the piano playing broken chords.

Debussy – Pour le piano: Sarabande

Background	• This work was composed in 1894 by the French composer Debussy.
	• It is the second of three movements that form the suite *Pour le piano*.
	• In the Baroque period, the sarabande was a slow piece (originally a dance) in triple time, with an emphasis on the second beat of the bar.
	• The Sarabande is Neoclassical: it reflects Debussy's interest in using earlier musical forms as the basis for composing in a much more modern style.
Rhythm and metre	• The movement is in slow triple metre ($\frac{3}{4}$), which is typical of the sarabande.
	• The emphasis on the second beat, shown by the placing of minims in bars 2, 4 and elsewhere, is also characteristic of the sarabande.
	• Descending patterns of quavers are beamed across the barlines in the middle section to emphasise their phrasing.
	• Hemiola-like cross rhythms appear in the final bars.
Melody	• Balanced phrases (e.g. bars 1–2 and 3–4) reflect the origins of the Sarabande as a dance.
	• Melodic ideas are often immediately repeated, sometimes with slight variations (such as in the first four bars).
	• The melody is formed from a combination of stepwise movement and small leaps.
	• The melody has a fairly restricted range until the final section.
Harmony	• Chords are non-functional, i.e. used for their colour rather than for their harmonic function of defining keys.
	• The harmony is often complex and chromatic. Characteristic features include:
	• Modal cadences
	• Parallelism applied to a range of chords
	• 9th and 13th chords
	• Half-diminished chords
	• Added 6th chords
	• Consecutive 5ths
	• Quartal harmony (chords based on superimposed 4ths).
Tonality	• The Sarabande is in the Aeolian mode, transposed to start on C♯.
	• The use of modal and quartal harmony leads to unusual cadences, such as the last two chords of the piece.
	• The tonality is ambiguous, clouded by features such as the use of the whole-tone scale in the bass.

Structure	• The movement has a rondo (or ternary) form (A–B–A1–C–A2–D–B1–coda).
	• Note that the opening section doesn't return in its original form…
	• …And further new material appears after its final return, ending with a short coda.
Resources and texture	• Debussy uses much of the piano's range, particularly in the lower register.
	• Most of the music requires the use of the sustaining pedal, particularly the spread chords (e.g. at the end where the final chord spans five octaves).
	• Textures include monophonic passages in bare octaves (such as bars 20–22), but are otherwise homophonic, including:
	• Six-part homorhythmic chords at the start
	• Parallel 4th chords (quartal harmony)
	• Parallel 6ths and parallel 7ths
	• Melody-dominated homophony.

VOCAL MUSIC 2014

Stravinsky – Symphony of Psalms: movement III

Background	• *Symphony of Psalms* was written to celebrate the 50th anniversary of the Boston Symphony Orchestra in 1930.
	• This movement is the last one in a three-movement work, and is a setting of Psalm 150 in Latin.
	• The work belongs to the second phase of Stravinsky's career, and is typified by:
	• An objective, unemotional approach
	• Neoclassicism
	• An unconventional use of language (e.g. splitting up words and displacing accents).
	• The work was intended for secular (non-religious) performance, in spite of its religious text.

Rhythm and metre	• The movement starts with a very slow opening section in $\frac{4}{4}$.
	• This section includes syncopations on the word 'Laudate', and a three-crotchet ostinato towards the end that is at odds with the prevailing pulse.
	• This is followed by a fast section that switches between $\frac{4}{4}$, $\frac{2}{2}$ and $\frac{3}{2}$, which includes:
	• A six-quaver motif, shifted to different beats
	• Triplets
	• Longer note lengths in the vocal parts
	• A slower section at bar 150 in $\frac{3}{2}$ with prominent dotted rhythms
	• A second slow section in $\frac{3}{2}$ at bar 163, which features a four-minim ostinato.
Melody and word setting	• Stravinsky avoids word-painting; instead the music is often soft, and doesn't use the instruments mentioned in the text (e.g. cymbals).
	• The vocal writing is mainly syllabic, with occasional melismas.
	• The syllables that make up a word are sometimes separated by rests (e.g. bars 70–71).
	• Stresses are often displaced, so they don't fall where you would naturally expect (e.g. the accent on 'Lau-' in bar 126).
	• The interval of a 3rd is significant throughout.
	• Most of the vocal melodies have a narrow range, revolving around the repetition of only a few notes, or even just the same note (such as the monotone six-quaver motif). This helps to give the music a Russian Orthodox flavour.
	• The narrow-range melodies contrast with the larger leaps and wider ranges in the slow, dotted-rhythms section (bars 150–162).
Harmony and tonality	• Though often triadic, the harmony is non-functional, lacking conventional cadences.
	• The movement begins and ends in C, although there is some ambiguity as to whether it is C major or C minor (both keys are suggested by the bitonality at the start of the movement).
	• There are modal elements in the music, e.g. the start could also suggest the Aeolian mode.
	• False relations contribute to the bitonality (e.g. E♭ and E♮ in bar 6).
	• Dissonances arise from the bitonality and added-note chords.
	• The slower section at bar 163 is in E♭.

Structure	• The movement is composed from a number of contrasting sections, some of which are repeated:
	• Slow introduction (Alleluia)
	• Fast section
	• Brief reference to the Alleluia
	• Reprise of the fast section
	• New slow section
	• A second new slow passage
	• Final reference to the Alleluia.
Resources	• Stravinsky excluded upper strings and clarinets in his attempt to create an objective, unemotional sound.
	• Much of the burden is taken by the woodwind and brass, notably:
	• 4 flutes and piccolo
	• 4 oboes and cor anglais
	• 3 bassoons and double bassoon
	• 4 horns in F
	• 1 trumpet in D
	• 4 trumpets in C
	• 3 trombones and tuba.
	• Other instruments are:
	• Timpani
	• Bass drum
	• Harp
	• 2 pianos
	• Cellos
	• Double bass.
	• Stravinsky writes for a four-part (SATB) choir (there are no soloists).
Texture	• Stravinsky combines his forces in various ways, for example:
	• Homophonic wind
	• Homophonic four-part choir
	• Tenors and basses in octaves (e.g. bars 175–182).
	• There is also some counterpoint, including imitation (for example in the slow section at bar 150).

Notice the transposing instruments. The piccolo plays an octave higher than written, the cor anglais and horns all play a 5th lower, and the trumpet in D plays a major 2nd higher.

Weelkes – Sing we at pleasure

Background	• This work was written in 1598 by the English composer Weelkes.
	• It is a ballett – a type of madrigal that was popular in the 16th and 17th centuries, characterised by a refrain set to the words 'fa la la'.
	• The work is secular and was intended for domestic performance.
Rhythm and metre	• The work is in a rapid triple metre ($\frac{3}{4}$) reflecting its dance-like nature.
	• Features include:
	• Dotted rhythms throughout
	• Syncopation (e.g. bar 12, alto)
	• Hemiola (e.g. bars 20–21).
Melody and word setting	• The word setting is almost entirely syllabic.
	• 'Fa la la' refrains intersperse the main text.
	• The melody consists largely of conjunct movement and small leaps, although there are a number of octave jumps (e.g. bar 2).
	• The lower voices have a wider range than the upper ones.
Harmony	• Although the music pre-dates the development of the major-minor tonal system, there are functional progressions, such as cadences.
	• The chords are all in root position or first inversion, and most of them are major.
	• Tonic and dominant chords are frequently alternated (such as in bars 19–22).
	• Notice the use of:
	• Suspensions (e.g. bar 83, alto)
	• The unusual interval of a diminished 5th (e.g. bar 10, C♯–G).
Tonality	• The work is in G major, briefly touching on D major and C major (although these modulations have no structural significance).
	• There are traces of (Mixolydian) modality in the F♮s.
Structure	• The work has a binary structure.
	• Each of the two sections is repeated, and finishes with a 'fa la la' refrain.
	• In the repeat of the second section (which is written out in full), the two sopranos swap parts.

Resources and texture	• The madrigal is written for five unaccompanied voices (SSATB). • The texture is largely contrapuntal, although there are brief passages of homophony (e.g. bars 31–34). • Weelkes uses various devices, including: • Imitation at different distances, from one beat to two bars, e.g.: 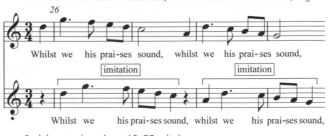 • Pedal notes (e.g. bars 46–52, alto).

Schubert – Der Doppelgänger

Background	• This work is a lied – a type of German song from the Romantic period. • It was composed in 1828 by the German composer Schubert, who is famous for having written hundreds of lieder. • For the text, Schubert set a poem by Heine, a well-known German poet.
Rhythm and metre	• The song is in a slow triple metre ($\frac{3}{4}$). • There are steady dotted-minim chords in the piano part almost throughout. • There are dotted rhythms in the vocal line.
Melody and word setting	• The word setting is mainly syllabic. • The longest melisma occurs at the end of the vocal part (bars 54–55). • The word setting largely adheres to the natural rhythms of the words, i.e. stronger syllables are stressed in the music as well. • The overall vocal range is a 13th (B–G). • Much of the melody consists of conjunct movement and small leaps, although there is a notable octave leap at the first climax. • Much of the vocal line revolves around F♯, particularly in the first half of the song. • The melody is broken up into short phrases, separated by rests. • A turn is used at bar 21, and there are occasional appoggiaturas (e.g. bar 35). • The first high point occurs at bar 31 (to accompany the words 'overwhelmed by pain'). • The melody rises even higher for the second climax at bar 41 ('my own face').

Harmony	• Striking harmonic features include:
	• The inner pedal on F♯ in the piano part (present throughout the first 40 bars, until the climax of the song).
	• Open 5th chords (e.g. bars 1 and 4).
	• Augmented 6th chords at the climaxes.
	• Chromaticism, particularly in the second half.
	• A Neapolitan chord in bar 59.
	• A plagal cadence and tierce de Picardie at the end.
Tonality	• The work is in B minor.
	• There is one modulation to the remote key of D♯ minor towards the end (bar 47).
Structure	• The work is through-composed.
	• There are three verses, with short linking passages in the piano between each one.
	• There is some repetition in the vocal line.
	• A four-bar ostinato-like figure in the piano is also repeated.
Resources and texture	• The song is written for tenor and piano.
	• The texture is melody-dominated homophony throughout.
	• The piano only takes the melody when the voice is silent.

Howlin' Wolf – I'm leavin' you

Background	• This song is an example of rhythm and blues.
	• It was recorded in 1958 for the album *Moanin' in the Moonlight*.
	• Howlin' Wolf (or Chester Burnett) was a black American blues singer, who also played guitar and harmonica.
Rhythm and metre	• The song is in a quadruple (common) metre (C), with swung quavers.
	• Features include:
	• An emphasised backbeat
	• Triplets in the piano part throughout most of the song
	• Semiquavers in the lead guitar part in bar 31, resulting in cross rhythms
	• Stop time.

Melody and word setting	• The vocal line is mostly syllabic, with a few short melismas.
	• The vocal range is a 10th (D–F).
	• There are irregular phrase lengths in the vocal line.
	• Much of the vocal phrases are based around a decorated, falling G minor triad.
	• The melody is primarily based on a G minor pentatonic scale.
	• The variations from verse to verse indicate improvisation.
Harmony and tonality	• The 12-bar blues progression is used throughout (based on chords I, IV and V).
	• There are frequent blue notes, which give the impression of G minor (even though the song is notated in G major).
	• 7th and 9th chords are also used throughout.
	• There is no modulation.
Structure	• There are six choruses of a 12-bar blues (i.e. the song is strophic).
	• These are framed by an introduction and coda (fade out).
Resources and texture	• The song is performed by voice, harmonica, lead and rhythm guitars, piano, bass and drums.
	• The texture is primarily melody-dominated homophony (interspersed with short passages of stop time).
	• The short introduction is largely monophonic.
	• There is dialogue between the voice and guitar.
	• Performance techniques include:
	• Pitch bends (e.g. bars 21–22, lead guitar)
	• Glissandos (e.g. bar 42, lead guitar)
	• Double-/triple-stopping in the lead guitar
	• Two- and three-chord notes in the harmonica.

Desmond Dekker and the Aces – You can get it if you really want

Background	• This song is an example of rocksteady (an early type of reggae).
	• It was written by the Jamaican musician Jimmy Cliff.
	• And recorded by the Jamaican singer Desmond Dekker in 1970.

Rhythm and metre	• The song is in a quadruple metre (**C**).
	• Features include:
	• The steady on-beat crotchets in the bass (typical of rocksteady)
	• An emphasis on the backbeat (characteristic of both rocksteady and reggae)
	• Syncopations in the upper parts
	• Triplets in the vocal parts
	• Drum fills.
Melody and word setting	• The word setting is mainly syllabic, with some melismas at the end of phrases.
	• The opening hook is repeated throughout the song.
	• The melody is mainly conjunct and narrow in range.
	• Although there are some high falsetto notes (e.g. bar 25).
	• The melody is largely confined to the notes of the major pentatonic scale.
Harmony and tonality	• The song is in D♭ major.
	• It is mainly based on just two chords: I (D♭) and IV (G♭).
	• Although the dominant 7th (A♭^{7}) also appears quite often.
	• There are more varied chords and a whole-tone scale in the short instrumental.
Structure	• The song is in verse-and-chorus form:
	• Intro
	• Chorus
	• Verse 1
	• Chorus
	• Verse 2
	• Chorus
	• Instrumental
	• Chorus
	• Outro
Resources and texture	• The texture is melody-dominated homophony, with:
	• Lead vocals
	• Backing vocals in two parts
	• Guitars and bass
	• Trumpets and saxes (sometimes playing in 3rds, which is typical of the style)
	• Electronic organ (an instrument commonly used in rocksteady and reggae)
	• Drums.

Sample questions 2014

Below you will find examples of the type of questions normally set in Section B of the exam. There are eight sample questions in total: two 10-mark questions and two 18-mark questions for the instrumental set works, and the same again for the vocal set works.

For each question, three sample answers are given: two that are marked already, as by an examiner, and one that you can mark for yourself. You should find that having a go at the questions yourself, and then comparing your answers to the ones given in this book, is an excellent way to revise for the exam, and will really help you to understand how to improve your marks.

INSTRUMENTAL MUSIC 2014

SAMPLE QUESTION 1

Describe the stylistic features of Brahms' Piano Quintet in F minor, Op. 34: movement III, which indicate that it was written in the Romantic era. (10)

Before reading any further, attempt the question yourself. You will find it useful to compare your own answer against the mark scheme (indicative content) and sample answers that follow.

> The expression 'indicative content' simply refers to the sort of information that examiners should look for when they are marking students' exam papers. It is not exhaustive and you may well gain marks for comments that are not included in the indicative content (providing of course that they are relevant and correct!).

Indicative content	
Structure	Scherzo and trio, with a basic ternary design for the trio; an expansion of the earlier minuet and trio.
Tonality	C minor ending in C major; extensive modulations.
Harmony	A wide harmonic vocabulary, drawing on chromatic chords, such as augmented 6ths and diminished 7ths; a preference for imperfect cadences; other devices include pedals, circle of 5ths, Phrygian cadence.
Melody	Prominent use of 3rds and broken-chord figuration; some motivic development; sequential repetition.
Rhythm and metre	Compound duple, with changes to simple time; syncopation; loose augmentation.
Texture	Considerable variation, embracing homophony and counterpoint (including fugato with five separate parts).
Instrumental writing	Thoroughly idiomatic; characteristically dense piano writing; strings both bowed and plucked; sometimes with a high tessitura; some double-stopping; octaves in the piano and strings.

Sample answer 1

The Brahms Quintet is a characteristic example of Romantic music, being completed only in 1865 after starting out as a string quintet a few years earlier. It clearly shows how instrumental techniques have improved down the ages as it requires considerable skill from the performer, with many of the string parts moving into the upper ranges [1] and requiring multiple stopping [1]. The piano part is also very demanding, as there are fast moving octaves and dense chords [1] very typical of this composer – Brahms was a notable piano virtuoso and gave over a hundred performances of the second of his piano concertos in the years immediately following its appearance.

In structure it is typical of the ternary scheme employed in the much earlier minuet and trio [1], but it is now massively expanded [1]. Like many later composers, Brahms moved away from the original three beats to the bar, increasing the speed of the music considerably and using compound duple $\frac{6}{8}$ [1], which on occasion is changed to $\frac{2}{4}$ [1]. This underlines the marked contrasts in the music, evident when he introduces the fugato [1] part way through the first section of the movement.

Here Brahms can demonstrate his skill in composing counterpoint, as it requires up to five independent parts [1]. It shows that although Brahms was a typical Romantic composer, he kept up his interest in earlier techniques.

Brahms uses a number of interesting harmonic techniques. Some are more typical of early music, such as the Phrygian cadence [1], but others are more Romantic, like the augmented 6th chords [1]. There are many modulations, one of the most dramatic coming with the sudden switch of key, which incidentally emphasises the sweeping rhythmic augmentation [1] near the beginning of the work.

> This final point in the paragraph is correct, but does not really add anything to the argument.

Examiner's points

The candidate made 12 points here that could gain a mark. Other references were rather imprecise. There is certainly evidence of strategic thinking in that there is an introduction with some attempt to provide context and the paragraphs follow a logical order. There are no errors of grammar or spelling, and the response is coherent, showing that the candidate is capable of producing a convincing, well-substantiated argument.

This answer would achieve a mark of 10/10.

Exercise

List additional points the candidate could have made, and find locations for the devices described.

Sample answer 2

The Romantic features are as follows:
- Structure – large scale

- The soaring melodies

- The rhythm – lots of dotted rhythms as opposed to smooth lines

- Tonality – the way it keeps changing instruments (see opening), going from single note on cello to full forces by end of page

- The instrumental writing which covers the whole range from very high to very low [1]

- The changing time signatures

- The lush harmonies

- The changing key signatures which can catch you out. It goes from F minor to C major [1] by the end of the piece. Obviously this makes it easier for the players

- The texture is thick.

Not enough information for a mark.

Not enough information for a mark.

The candidate has confused dotted rhythms with staccato here.

The candidate has confused tonality with tone quality or timbre.

Not enough information for a mark.

Avoid unhelpful descriptions such as this. The term 'lush' tells us nothing useful about the type of chords used.

Although the *complete* work is described as being in F minor, this movement starts in C minor. The notion that music in C major is 'easier' is, of course, nonsensical.

This is another unhelpful description.

Examiner's points

There were really only two creditworthy points here. There was one near miss, where the candidate referred to 'large-scale' structure, but it was a pity that more specific information about the links with the minuet or the ternary scheme of the trio was not given. There were significant weaknesses, noted in the margin boxes.

Holistically, it would be impossible to award more than 2/10. The answer was comprehensible, but there was no organisation or argument. Spelling was correct, but the grammar used to express each point was sometimes poor.

Exercise

Rewrite the above answer in complete sentences, replacing unhelpful or uninformative remarks with specific details.

Sample answer 3

Mark this answer yourself, commenting at the end on its good points but also mentioning ways in which it could have been improved. Check your assessment against the examiner's comments that follow, after completing your marking.

Brahms' Scherzo and Trio from the Piano Quintet in F minor is typical of his essentially Romantic approach. Brahms was something of a traditionalist, following deliberately in the footsteps of Beethoven, and so it is not surprising to find that he often uses an enlarged version of the Minuet and Trio introduced by Haydn into multi-movement works. There is now no trace of the original rather refined dance. Instead this is a fast movement, mainly in compound duple time, though some sections are in simple $\frac{2}{4}$ time (the sort of change that was unheard of in earlier Classical times).

Although the movement is in an overall ternary form (ABA), with the central section also in a smaller version of ternary form, there are no repeats, but instead a steadily developing structure. In this respect, the extensive modulations play a vital role in maintaining momentum and interest. The movement opens in C minor with a tonic pedal on cello and a rising arpeggiated theme. With the first change of time signature comes the second motif which will be extensively used throughout the movement. Immediately Brahms augments it, then switches it from C minor to C major.

As the movement goes on, Brahms uses many more keys, notably Eb minor at the start of the fugato, changing to major at the climax of this section. In contrast, the Trio is in C major, touching briefly on B major and making use of a circle of 5ths.

In addition, Brahms draws on a fairly large range of harmonies, frequently featuring the augmented 6th to dominant progression. Such chromatic harmony is a regular feature of Romantic writing, especially in Wagner.

Perhaps the most significant feature of this work to point to the Romantic era is the wide variety of textures and the advanced instrumental techniques employed. Brahms does not use much in the way of special effects, such as advanced bowing techniques and harmonics, but he uses double-stopping fairly frequently and often takes the strings up into very high registers. He also effectively contrasts pizzicato and bowed strings. The piano writing is typically complicated with many octave passages or strings of dense chords. The textures range from octaves on strings to counterpoint for all instruments in the fugato. At other points, Brahms also uses homophony for the entire ensemble.

It is sometimes difficult to isolate the purely Romantic features in Brahms' work because he was so influenced by earlier composers, but the Scherzo and Trio is truly Romantic in its expansion of Classical forms, its textures and instrumental techniques, and to a degree, its harmonic and tonal methods.

Examiner's points

There is plenty to credit in this answer, for example:

- Enlarged minuet and trio scheme
- Compound and simple duple time signatures
- Ternary form in the trio
- Modulation
- C minor, C major, E♭ minor located at the start of the fugato and E♭ major at the climax
- Tonic pedal and arpeggiated theme at the start
- Augmentation
- Circle of 5ths in the trio
- Chromatic harmony and use of augmented 6th chords
- Wide variety of textures and idiomatic writing
- Double-stopping, high registers, pizzicato and bowed strings
- Octaves in strings and piano
- Dense piano chords
- Counterpoint in the fugato
- Homophony.

The answer was well planned and organised, with a good introduction and conclusion. There were no spelling or grammar errors. More than enough points were made to gain full marks.

Exercise

Memorise as many of the points above as you can, then write your own answer, allowing yourself no more than 25 minutes. You may write in either note form or continuous prose.

SAMPLE QUESTION 2

Describe those features of the Sarabande from _Pour le piano_ which are typical of Debussy's style. (10)

Before reading any further, attempt the question yourself. You will find it useful to compare your own answer against the mark scheme (indicative content) and sample answers that follow.

Indicative content	
Melody	Modal, Aeolian on C#; repetition of one and two-bar phrases with little variation.
Harmony	Non-functional, with modal cadences; chromatic chords (such as half-diminished); quartal harmony; consecutive 5ths. Parallelism applied to a range of different chords.
Tonality	Ambiguous/non-functional; whole-tone elements.
Texture	Homophony; octaves; range of densities; some spread chords; sustaining pedal essential; wide range used.
Genre and rhythm	Neoclassical sarabande; frequent emphasis on the second beat; some cross-phrasing; hemiola.
Structure	The structure can be described as ternary or rondo.

Sample answer 1

Debussy's style is one of the most easily recognised and individual.

First, there is the fact that it is strongly modal [1], revolving around C# Aeolian [1]. The melody often consists of two-bar phrases, simply repeated [1], while the rhythm also involves many repeated patterns. Because it is a sarabande, Debussy uses a clear rhythmic pattern here which often leads to stresses on the second beat, e.g. the frequent minims [1]. He also uses triplets and dotted rhythms, and frequent tied notes going over the barline.

One of the most striking features of Debussy's style is the way he uses harmony and tonality, which is often a bit vague, partly because of the use of whole-tone effects [1]. This is an artificial scale in which all the notes are exactly a tone apart. This means that there can only be six notes in each octave, e.g. C D E F# Ab Bb, or else C# D# F G A B. If you try to form chords from this scale,

> This is true, but these features are to be found in the work of many other composers.

> 'A bit vague' is not specific enough for a mark.

you can only produce augmented triads, or even more dissonant effects. Debussy came across this scale in Russia when he worked there for a short while in the 19th century. Rimsky Korsakov often used it. Actually there is no whole-tone harmony as such in the sarabande, though the bass moves around by whole-tone step. The chords above it are ordinary and can be formed from normal scales. What is unusual about this passage is that you end up with a stream of 7th chords in parallel motion [1], and that is one of the most typical features of Debussy's style.

In fact, there is lots of parallelism throughout this piece which produces some very interesting effects. Its a pity we are not supposed to use it in the harmony question on this paper!

◄ Missing apostrophe in the word 'It's'.

Examiner's points

There are six creditworthy points here. Unfortunately, there are also irrelevant points and a general lack of focus. The organisation needs to be tighter. There is, for example, the excessively long explanation of the whole-tone scale, and the response would have benefited from a conclusion.

A mark of 5/10 is appropriate.

Exercise

Prune the answer, removing any irrelevance. Provide a brief conclusion.

Sample answer 2

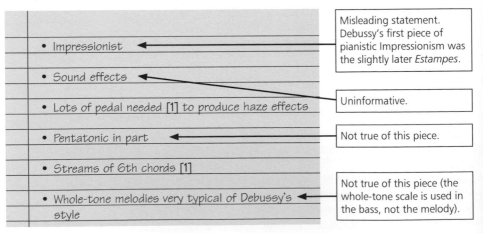

- Impressionist ◄

  Misleading statement. Debussy's first piece of pianistic Impressionism was the slightly later *Estampes*.

- Sound effects ◄

  Uninformative.

- Lots of pedal needed [1] to produce haze effects

- Pentatonic in part ◄

  Not true of this piece.

- Streams of 6th chords [1]

- Whole-tone melodies very typical of Debussy's ◄ style

  Not true of this piece (the whole-tone scale is used in the bass, not the melody).

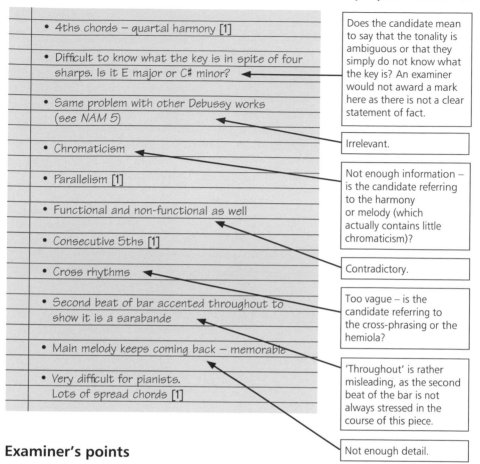

- 4ths chords – quartal harmony [1]

Does the candidate mean to say that the tonality is ambiguous or that they simply do not know what the key is? An examiner would not award a mark here as there is not a clear statement of fact.

- Difficult to know what the key is in spite of four sharps. Is it E major or C# minor?

- Same problem with other Debussy works (see NAM 5)

Irrelevant.

- Chromaticism

Not enough information – is the candidate referring to the harmony or melody (which actually contains little chromaticism)?

- Parallelism [1]

- Functional and non-functional as well

- Consecutive 5ths [1]

Contradictory.

- Cross rhythms

Too vague – is the candidate referring to the cross-phrasing or the hemiola?

- Second beat of bar accented throughout to show it is a sarabande

- Main melody keeps coming back – memorable

'Throughout' is rather misleading, as the second beat of the bar is not always stressed in the course of this piece.

- Very difficult for pianists. Lots of spread chords [1]

Examiner's points

Not enough detail.

There were six not very well-focused points made here. You can answer any of these questions in note form or bullet points if you wish, but you should take care to make your observations as clear as possible.

Exercise

Rearrange the previous answer, expanding the statements to make complete sentences. Group the ideas together, so that the answer gains coherence.

Sample answer 3

Mark this answer yourself, commenting at the end on its good points, but also mentioning ways in which it could have been improved. Check your assessment against the examiner's comments that follow, after completing your marking.

Debussy was one of the most revolutionary composers in the history of music, and did much to pave the way for the development of 20th-century music. In fact, Boulez has stated that 20th-century music began with *Prélude à l'après-midi d'un faune*.

The Sarabande, composed in 1894, not much later than the *Prélude*, came from the suite *Pour le piano*, and like *Suite bergamasque*, also composed at this time, is an early example of Neoclassicism. Here Debussy deliberately refers back to the styles and methods of earlier periods. It was an approach adopted throughout his career, some of his final works being the sonatas for various combinations of instruments. In the Sarabande, the rhythms are typical of this type of dance, with the second beat of the bar emphasised, often by having a minim placed on it (as in the second bar). The rhythm is not as varied as it is in some other works by Debussy, though he also introduces hemiola near the end.

The more typical aspects of his work are evident in the melody, harmony and tonality. The work is based on the Aeolian mode on C#. A typical feature of Debussy's style is the use of repeated phrases. This can clearly be seen at the opening, with the first two bars immediately repeated with the addition of a passing note.

Debussy's harmony is also very typical in this piece. There is much parallelism, involving almost every type of chord, such as 5ths and complete triads. He also uses streams of parallel 7ths, and even longer streams of 6th chords. The most original harmony occurs with the use of 4th chords:

The result is that at this point of the piece it is almost impossible to analyse the key, resulting in non-functional tonality.

These are the aspects which make Debussy's music so original.

Examiner's points

There were enough points here to gain full marks:

- Neoclassicism, sarabande rhythm (and location), hemiola
- Aeolian mode on C#
- Repetition of melody and example
- Parallelism of 6ths, triads and 7th chords
- Quartal harmony
- Non-functional tonality.

There were some good, if rather over-extended, introductory remarks establishing the historical context, but a less convincing conclusion. You may feel that even though this answer would have gained ten marks, it could be improved by focusing more directly on the music, and by introducing references to texture and structure. Notice that no additional marks were awarded for the musical example as the candidate used an incorrect clef, missed out the key signature and gave an incorrect chord.

Exercise

Improve the response above by taking out any information you consider inessential, and by writing a brief conclusion.

SAMPLE QUESTION 3

Compare and contrast the resources and textures of Pavane 'The image of melancholy' and Galliard 'Ecce quam bonum' by Holborne with Sarabande from *Pour le piano* by Debussy. (18)

Before reading any further, attempt the question yourself. You will find it useful to compare your own answer against the mark scheme (indicative content) and sample answers that follow.

Indicative content	
Resources	**Holborne**: written for viols or violins, and/or wind instruments; derived from vocal styles (unidiomatic).
	Typically played by a single family of instruments, resulting in little variation of timbre.
	Debussy: written for solo piano; sustaining pedal essential.
Textures	**Holborne**: five-part texture; mainly contrapuntal; central passage of the Galliard is more homophonic.
	Imitation and inversion is used in both dances.
	Pedal notes are used in the bass; the bass line in general is less active than the other parts.
	Debussy: mainly homophonic, opening with chords in six parts; some use of melody-dominated homophony; octaves used at various pitches.
	Spread chords.
	Homophonic textures employ much parallelism.

Sample answer 1

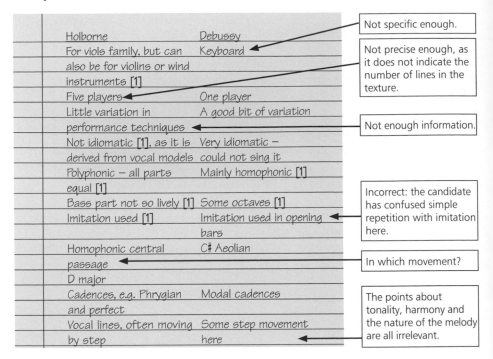

Holborne	Debussy
For viols family, but can also be for violins or wind instruments [1]	Keyboard
Five players	One player
Little variation in performance techniques	A good bit of variation
Not idiomatic [1], as it is derived from vocal models	Very idiomatic – could not sing it
Polyphonic – all parts equal [1]	Mainly homophonic [1]
Bass part not so lively [1]	Some octaves [1]
Imitation used [1]	Imitation used in opening bars
Homophonic central passage	C♯ Aeolian
D major	
Cadences, e.g. Phrygian and perfect	Modal cadences
Vocal lines, often moving by step	Some step movement here

Annotations:
- Not specific enough.
- Not precise enough, as it does not indicate the number of lines in the texture.
- Not enough information.
- Incorrect: the candidate has confused simple repetition with imitation here.
- In which movement?
- The points about tonality, harmony and the nature of the melody are all irrelevant.

Examiner's points

At most this answer would gain 7/18, although marks may be deducted for the lack of organisation, and the vague or irrelevant statements. If you decide to compare and contrast using columns, as in this answer, you need to be careful to avoid making inappropriate or negative contrasts (for example, describing one work as being contrapuntal and the other work as being 'not contrapuntal' – negative statements such as this are unlikely to gain you any marks). There is also the risk that an answer written in brief notes or bullet points may lack clarity and coherence.

Exercise

Rewrite the answer, removing irrelevance, grouping related points together and writing in sentences, however short, to clarify the meaning.

Sample answer 2

The works by Holborne and Debussy come from totally
different periods, the Holborne being a product of
the English Renaissance, and the Debussy a piece
by a French composer working three centuries
later. Not surprisingly, these differences are clearly
reflected in their works, both of them being stylised
dances. Holborne's work is a typically refined Pavane
and Galliard, its complexity indicating that it was
never really intended for dancing. It is a five-part [1],
mainly contrapuntal [1] work, all parts being of equal
importance [1]. The parts themselves may be played by
viols [1], though the composer said it did not matter
much whether the pieces were performed by violins,
winds or even the broken (mixed) consort often used
at this time. The point was that it was possible to
perform this music on almost anything that was
around as the parts were vocal-derived and thus not
instrumentally idiomatic [1]. The five-part polyphony
makes for a complex texture, as is evident in the
imitations [1] and inversions [1]. Only the bass part is
a little less lively [1], with the occasional pedal note [1].
The one significant break from counterpoint comes in
the central passage of the Galliard [1 for location of
the following observation] which is homophonic [1].

The Debussy Sarabande is completely different.
This is obviously intended for performance on the piano
[1], and could not be played on anything else as the
sustaining pedal is essential [1]. Whereas contrasts
of timbre were almost non-existent in the Holborne [1], ◄── Notice the construction
Debussy is able to obtain many variations on the piano | of this sentence, in
by using different registers, such as the low octaves | which the opening
[1] at the end of the first main section [1 for location], | word 'whereas' sets up
the gloomy 4ths chords which follow [1], which contrast | a contrasting of ideas.
again with the higher streams of 6ths chords [1]. At
other times the full range of the keyboard is used [1],
e.g. the final chord [1 for example]. In marked contrast
to the Holborne, there is no counterpoint as such, this
movement being totally homophonic [1], or else melody
and chordal accompaniment [1] – aside from the octave
passages already mentioned. Debussy is still able
to vary the textures enormously – from the six-part
chords [1] at the start [1 for location] to the massive
spread chords [1] at the climax.

Examiner's points

25 points were made, ensuring a very high overall mark. In terms of organisation, the contrast worked well, with the differences between the two works becoming clear as the response proceeded. The one disappointing aspect is the absence of a conclusion.

Exercise

Provide a brief conclusion (20–25 words) for the answer above. You may find it helpful to make reference to the remarks in the opening paragraph.

Sample answer 3

Mark this answer yourself, commenting at the end on its good points, but also mentioning ways in which it could have been improved. Check your assessment against the examiner's comments that follow, after completing your marking.

With Holborne's Pavane, the texture is broken chords, which is quite thin. The use of a lot of minims gives the thin texture because most of the instruments are playing long notes, such as minims and semibreves. There is more of a texture when there are crotchets and quavers – as in the Debussy. The longest notes, which are often tied together, come in the bass part, giving pedal notes. Pedals come in the Debussy as well, but these are devices in the piano to help sustain the sound. It saves having to hang on to the note so you can carry on doing something different. The middle section of the Holborne Galliard has a different texture as all the notes seem to come together giving chords.

The Holborn is written for more instruments than the Debussy, but the composer did not mind which were used so long as people bought his music. In fact, that's probably why he was so vague so people who played viles, violins or wind instruments would all want to buy it, whereas Debussy could only sell his music to keyboard players, and there aren't that many around as it takes too long to learn.

With Debussy, the texture is sometimes thick and sometimes thin. In fact he gets a lot of variety into the Sarabande this way. He uses six notes at the start which places great emphasis on the tonality, but also rich textures that can easily be contrasted with thinner passages like octaves. That type of sparse texture contrasts to what went before, but almost immediately, Debussy is back to using a lot more notes. Some of his chords are moved around in blocks so he ends up with consecutives.

Both Holborne and Debussy create variety by using contrasting textures.

Examiner's points

You may well have felt that this answer should have carried a health warning as it is more a lesson in how not to do it. But, in spite of all its nonsensical assertions and confusions, not to mention spelling errors, it would have gained some credit for:

• Pedal notes in the Holborne
• Chords (with location) in the Galliard
• Debussy's use of octaves, chords and consecutives.

The flaws include a real confusion as to what texture involves (the references to rhythmic values being irrelevant and misleading), the unhelpful asides about the sustaining pedal and the irrelevancies regarding sales of music.

It would gain 6/18, as a very basic answer.

Exercise

Extract the few valid points the candidate made and add further observations to bring the mark up to around 16–17/18.

SAMPLE QUESTION 4

Compare and contrast rhythm and melody in Symphony No. 26 in D minor, 'Lamentatione': movement I by Haydn and Piano Quintet in F minor, Op. 34: movement III by Brahms. (18)

Before reading any further, attempt the question yourself. You will find it useful to compare your own answer against the mark scheme (indicative content) and sample answers that follow.

Indicative content	
Rhythm and metre	**Haydn**: simple quadruple/four beats to the bar; syncopation; constant quaver movement in the second-subject countermelody. **Brahms**: compound duple/two dotted crotchets to the bar, switching to simple duple/two beats on occasion; syncopation; cross rhythms; augmentation.
Melody	**Haydn**: first subject in a minor key, with periodic phrasing; second subject in a major key, based on plainsong, with modal inflections, and mainly conjunct movement; ornamentation, including appoggiaturas. **Brahms**: first and second themes in a minor key, third theme in a major key; broken-chord patterns; motivic links between themes; sequential repetition; fragmentation; various phrase lengths.

Sample answer 1

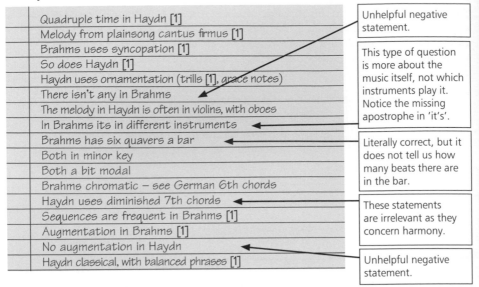

Quadruple time in Haydn [1]	Unhelpful negative statement.
Melody from plainsong cantus firmus [1]	
Brahms uses syncopation [1]	This type of question is more about the music itself, not which instruments play it. Notice the missing apostrophe in 'it's'.
So does Haydn [1]	
Haydn uses ornamentation (trills [1], grace notes)	
There isn't any in Brahms	
The melody in Haydn is often in violins, with oboes	
In Brahms its in different instruments	
Brahms has six quavers a bar	Literally correct, but it does not tell us how many beats there are in the bar.
Both in minor key	
Both a bit modal	
Brahms chromatic – see German 6th chords	
Haydn uses diminished 7th chords	These statements are irrelevant as they concern harmony.
Sequences are frequent in Brahms [1]	
Augmentation in Brahms [1]	
No augmentation in Haydn	Unhelpful negative statement.
Haydn classical, with balanced phrases [1]	

Examiner's points

This answer would gain 8/18. Some basic points are made here, but in a rather clumsy manner. Answers in note form are perfectly acceptable, but the points still have to be organised and grouped so as to result in a coherent answer. Avoid redundant balancing statements in which one side is entirely negative, such as 'Haydn uses trills, Brahms doesn't.'

Exercise

Organise the answer above, omitting irrelevant or negative remarks, grouping points together, and expanding the original observations to form complete sentences for the sake of clarity.

Sample answer 2

Haydn's work is highly typical of this phase of his writing, the stormy atmosphere being characteristic of the *Sturm und Drang* style, while Brahms was a Romantic who drew on classical models.	Good basic introduction.
The storm and stress of Haydn's music comes through in the fast four beats to the bar [1] and syncopations [1]. Brahms' music is also fast and	

furious, with syncopation [1]. In contrast to Haydn, he
uses two dotted beats a bar [1].

    The classical side of Haydn's writing is obvious in
the periodic phrasing [1], especially in the first subject –
the opening 16 bars [1 for location]. Brahms also uses
four-bar phrases [1] – at the opening of the fugato, for
example [1 for location].

    Haydn uses both minor and major modes for his
melodies [1] and there are touches of modality [1] at
times in the second subject [1 for location]. Brahms
also uses a mixture of major and minor [1]. ◄

> Note that you can gain
> marks in a question
> on 'melody' for
> specifying the tonality
> of the melodies (this
> is not just information
> you need to save for
> questions specifically
> on harmony or
> tonality).

Examiner's points

This answer would gain 12/18. Its introductory remarks provided some useful background, but the main part of the response was rather randomly organised and lacked both vital information on Brahms' melodic writing and a conclusion.

Exercise

Reorganise the answer, grouping points together to create a more coherent response. Suggest additional points that could be included, and write a brief conclusion.

Sample answer 3

Mark this answer yourself, commenting at the end on its good points, but also mentioning ways in which it could have been improved. Check your assessment against the examiner's comments that follow, after completing your marking.

    Approximately a century separates the writing of the symphony by
Haydn and the quintet by Brahms, and obviously music improved
tremendously during that period. Much of this was due to the
developments which took place in the instruments available. Haydn could
only draw on the hand horn and harpsichord, and so was limited in what
he could write. In contrast, Brahms had a grand piano and virtuoso
string players.

    Haydn's symphony is in a basic sonata form, opening in D minor with
the first subject typified by driving syncopations. In contrast, the second
subject in F major has non-stop quavers, though this is an ornamental
part as the real melody here is the plainchant line, which typically moves
by step. Haydn had to take away the free rhythms typical of this early
music, and make it fit the four beats to a bar time signature. The entire
movement is based on these two ideas.

In contrast, there is considerable variety in the Brahms. Here the signature is compound duple and, like Haydn, Brahms uses syncopation right from the start where the violins' opening idea is set against the steady repeated note in the cello. This first idea is an arpeggiated climbing melody, rising by sequence. With the change of time signature to $\frac{2}{4}$ another important theme is introduced with repeated notes and a motif that revolves around the dominant. Brahms immediately augments this idea, and it is heard at the same time in heterophony in the viola part. Next we have full chordal homophony, switched into C major with dramatic effect.

All these devices are used throughout, e.g. sequences appear in the trio's main theme as well.

Examiner's points

The candidate offered much relevant information:

- First subject of Haydn in D minor, with syncopations (and location)
- Second subject in F major, with continuous quavers (and location)
- Use of mainly conjunct plainchant, modified to fit $\frac{4}{4}$
- Compound duple in Brahms
- Syncopation (and location) as well as arpeggiation and rising sequence
- Change to duple time, the repeated-note figure, augmentation and major mode.

Even though the number of observations made would secure a high mark, the response could have been significantly improved. The opening remarks are contentious (i.e. the notion that music improves as time goes on) and irrelevant, as were the references to textures. The response fades away, and would have benefited from a more substantial conclusion.

Exercise

Redraft the introduction and write a brief conclusion emphasising the similarities between the two works.

VOCAL MUSIC 2014

SAMPLE QUESTION 1

Describe the stylistic features of Weelkes' *Sing we at pleasure* **which show that this work is an example of Renaissance music. (10)**

Before reading any further, attempt the question yourself. You will find it useful to compare your own answer against the mark scheme (indicative content) and sample answers that follow.

Indicative content	
Genre	Ballett (a type of madrigal), typified by fa-la refrains.
Rhythm	Lively triple metre; dotted rhythms; syncopation; hemiola.
Melody	Major with modal F♯s; melody largely consists of steps/small leaps, but some jumps of an octave; word setting is almost entirely syllabic.
Harmony	Root-position and first-inversion chords; frequent alternation of tonic and dominant chords; suspensions; diminished 5ths.
Texture	Mainly five-part counterpoint, with imitations at one-bar and two-bar distances; brief homophony.
Structure	Two sections, repeated; each finishing with a fa-la refrain.

Sample answer 1

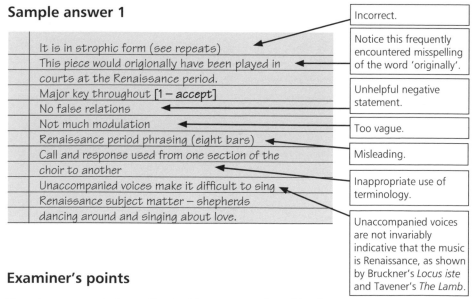

It is in strophic form (see repeats)

This piece would origionally have been played in courts at the Renaissance period.

Major key throughout [1 – accept]

No false relations

Not much modulation

Renaissance period phrasing (eight bars)

Call and response used from one section of the choir to another

Unaccompanied voices make it difficult to sing

Renaissance subject matter – shepherds dancing around and singing about love.

Incorrect.

Notice this frequently encountered misspelling of the word 'originally'.

Unhelpful negative statement.

Too vague.

Misleading.

Inappropriate use of terminology.

Unaccompanied voices are not invariably indicative that the music is Renaissance, as shown by Bruckner's *Locus iste* and Tavener's *The Lamb*.

Examiner's points

There is one correct observation in this answer, so it could only be awarded 1/10.

Exercise

Cut out the irrelevant and unhelpful remarks. Rewrite the remaining statements in sentences. Without referring to your notes, see how many valid points you can add.

Sample answer 2

Sing we at pleasure is a characteristic piece of English Renaissance music. It is a type of madrigal, known as a ballett [1], and as such is typified by the fa-la refrains [1], coming at the end of each of its two sections [1]. Each of these sections is repeated [1], the second with some voice exchange [1]. Its word setting is syllabic [1] and it has a lively, dancing three beats to the bar [1] to help emphasise the sense of the text. It has no key signature, but it is clearly in G major [1], with the occasional F♮ giving a Mixolydian feel [1].

Other stylistic features typical of Renaissance music include the harmony, built largely on root position and first inversion chords [1], with frequent dominant to tonic progressions [1], while the textures are mainly contrapuntal [1], with imitations between the various parts [1].

Examiner's points

This is an example of good, efficient writing and would gain 10/10.

Exercise

List the additional creditworthy points the candidate could have made about texture.

Sample answer 3

Mark this answer yourself, commenting at the end on its good points, but also mentioning ways in which it could have been improved. Check your assessment against the examiner's comments that follow, after completing your marking.

Sing we at pleasure sounds like Renaissance music being for five unaccompanied voices, like much of the religious music of the period. Intended for amateurs at a time when all educated people were expected to be able to read and sing music. It is a typical madrigal, a type of music imported from Italy, in this case taking the form of a ballett. Typical features include the refrain, which breaks up the through-composed structure, and the text about singing and dancing.

This music is very regular, and is in the same sort of style throughout. It is also quite difficult to describe as it has parts for five

different voices. Some of the voices are independent, or rather they are
doing the same thing but at different times, like the opening where the
top parts come in with the same idea, but the second one a bar later.
There is also quite a bit of off-beat singing here, all of which is
typical, giving us some idea of the music of the Renaissance period.

Examiner's points

There are at most four creditworthy observations here: five voices, ballett, refrain and the rather convoluted description of imitation.* There was some irrelevance ('amateur performance'), repetition ('five voices') and misleading statements ('very regular' and 'off-beat singing'). Notice the incomplete sentence in the first paragraph, and the overuse of the word 'typical'.

*This shows why it is so important to know the correct terms and be able to use them.

Exercise

With the aim of doubling the candidate's mark, cut out both the irrelevant and misleading statements, then supplement what is left with one additional point for each of the following aspects: structure, harmony, texture and rhythm.

SAMPLE QUESTION 2

Describe the features of *Symphony of Psalms*: movement III that are characteristic of Stravinsky's style. (10)

Before reading any further, attempt the question yourself. You will find it useful to compare your own answer against the mark scheme (indicative content) and sample answers that follow.

Indicative content	
Rhythm	Displaced accents; some changes of metre; dotted rhythms; use of ostinati.
Melody	Some narrow-range melodies, reflecting Russian Orthodox influences; monotone lines; some melodies with wider ranges.
Word setting	Unexpected interpretation of the text; mainly syllabic; syllables broken up by rests ('hocket').
Harmony	Non-functional; bitonality; false relations.
Tonality	C minor/major at the beginning and end; E♭ for the slower section near the end; modal elements (such as Aeolian at the start).
Texture	Some homophony; some counterpoint, including imitation; orchestra lacking upper strings and clarinets.
Context	Religious text but intended for secular performance; Neoclassical.

Sample answer 1

Symphony of Psalms was written to celebrate the 50th anniversary of the foundation of the Boston Symphony Orchestra (1930), and so dates from the neoclassical phase [1] of Stravinsky's career (as opposed to the earlier nationalist phase and the later serialist period). In seeking to create an objective, unemotional style, he excluded the upper strings [1] in favour of more reeds and brass instruments, as well as two pianos. His approach to the text is unusual, as he does not use any percussion other than timps and so ◄── does not illustrate cymbals to underline the sense of the words [1]. Other strange aspects include the slow, quiet setting of the final section of the psalm [1].

> It is not true to say that Stravinsky only uses timpani as he also includes a part for bass drum.

Although the work is not obviously nationalist, there are traces of Russian Orthodox church music [1], notably the narrow-range melodies [1]. They are also modal, e.g. at the start with the Aeolian mode [1]. At other points, Stravinsky uses monotone lines (Laudate Dominum) [1], and here he introduces rests which sound rather like the medieval hocket [1]. The six-note monotone lines — the repeated quavers — are often rhythmically displaced [1].

Other melodies have a much wider range [1], notably the theme treated like a canon [1] with dotted rhythms [1].

Like many of Stravinsky's neoclassical works, this has strong tonal elements, beginning and ending on C [1]. Other passages show traces of bitonality [1].

Symphony of Psalms is undoubtedly the work of Stravinsky for the reasons mentioned, though it has a much more regular rhythmic scheme compared with *Rite of Spring*.

Examiner's points

This answer would achieve 10/10, with a good introduction and an attempt at a conclusion.

Exercise

Introduce a paragraph on texture, largely neglected by the candidate, and write a more comprehensive concluding paragraph.

Sample answer 2

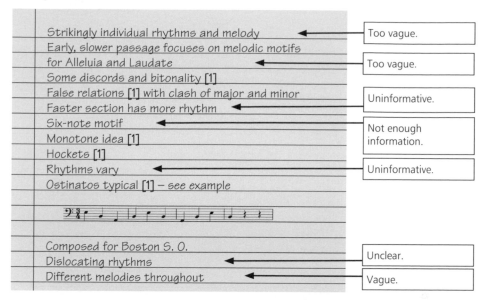

Strikingly individual rhythms and melody — Too vague.

Early, slower passage focuses on melodic motifs
for Alleluia and Laudate — Too vague.

Some discords and bitonality [1]

False relations [1] with clash of major and minor — Uninformative.

Faster section has more rhythm —

Six-note motif — Not enough information.

Monotone idea [1]

Hockets [1]

Rhythms vary — Uninformative.

Ostinatos typical [1] – see example

Composed for Boston S. O.

Dislocating rhythms — Unclear.

Different melodies throughout — Vague.

Examiner's points

This answer would likely gain 5/10, although could potentially be deducted a mark for its poor quality of writing. No point would be awarded for the music example, as it uses the wrong time signature and lacks a key signature.

> ### Exercise
>
> Try improving this response by cutting out the irrelevant and vague comments, and by adding at least a further three points, one each on melody, text-setting and texture. Write complete sentences, and group the points together for extra coherence.

Sample answer 3

Mark this answer yourself, commenting at the end on its good points, but also mentioning ways in which it could have been improved. Check your assessment against the examiner's comments that follow, after completing your marking.

> Symphony of Psalms was written to celebrate the 50th anniversary of the Boston Symphony Orchestra. It is a typical piece from Stravinsky's middle, neoclassical period.
>
> The neoclassical element is more to do with traditional elements of musical style being brought into the 20th century.
>
> There are both tonal passages and bitonal sections.
>
> There are ostinatos, giving a steady pulse and also a basic framework – see the slow passage at the end with its ostinato.
>
> There are some rhythms played staccato to create tension and drama. They build up suspense, e.g. motif e.
>
> There are typical snatches of Russian folk music; often they are narrow in range.
>
> Orchestration is unusual – there are more trumpets and oboes than expected, but no strings or percussion.
>
> There are modal elements. In the slower passage at the opening there is a problem working out whether the melody is in C minor or E♭, or whether it is in Aeolian C minor. Probably it is Aeolian.
>
> There are false relations, when C major and minor clash.
>
> There is unusual text setting. There are no cymbals when the words refer to loud cymbals.

Examiner's points

There are eight creditworthy points in this response:

- Neoclassical
- Bitonality
- Ostinati (with the location)
- Narrow-range melodies
- Aeolian
- False relations
- No cymbals.

This answer is obviously better than the previous one, but it suffers from slack expressions, incomplete statements and an overuse of 'There are …' to open sentences. It referred to motif 'e' without establishing where it occurs; gave the impression that there were no strings at all in the orchestra; and took too long to establish that the Aeolian mode was used.

Exercise

Improve this answer by organising it into longer paragraphs consisting of related facts, building on the incomplete statements as necessary.

SAMPLE QUESTION 3

Compare and contrast melody and word setting in Schubert's *Der Doppelgänger* and Stravinsky's *Symphony of Psalms*. (18)

Before reading any further, attempt the question yourself. You will find it useful to compare your own answer against the mark scheme (indicative content) and sample answers that follow.

Indicative content	
Melody	**Schubert**: in a minor key; initially revolves around an F♯; overall range of a 13th; short phrases separated by rests; appoggiaturas, turn; mainly conjunct with small leaps, though an octave jump at the first climax; moves to higher registers for the climaxes. **Stravinsky**: broad contrast between narrow- and wide-range melodies; also between conjunct writing and larger intervals; modality; chromaticism; melodies often revolve around just a few notes; some use of monotone ideas; ostinati.
Word setting	**Schubert**: mainly syllabic, but with a long melisma at the end; speech and musical accents coincide; climaxes underline the poet's pain and sighting of his ghostly double. **Stravinsky**: syllables are sometimes split up; unexpected interpretation of the text; accents are often displaced; mainly syllabic.

Sample answer 1

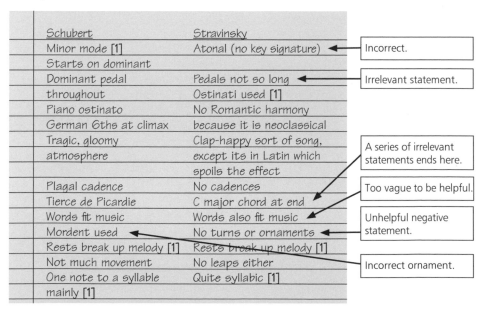

Schubert	Stravinsky	
Minor mode [1]	Atonal (no key signature)	← Incorrect.
Starts on dominant		
Dominant pedal throughout	Pedals not so long	← Irrelevant statement.
Piano ostinato	Ostinati used [1]	
German 6ths at climax	No Romantic harmony because it is neoclassical	
Tragic, gloomy atmosphere	Clap-happy sort of song, except its in Latin which spoils the effect	A series of irrelevant statements ends here.
Plagal cadence	No cadences	
Tierce de Picardie	C major chord at end	Too vague to be helpful.
Words fit music	Words also fit music	Unhelpful negative statement.
Mordent used	No turns or ornaments	Incorrect ornament.
Rests break up melody [1]	Rests break up melody [1]	
Not much movement	No leaps either	
One note to a syllable mainly [1]	Quite syllabic [1]	

Examiner's points

This answer would gain a mark of 6/10. The candidate was not concentrating on the demands of the question.

> ## Exercise
>
> Rewrite and supplement the valid statements to earn the candidate more marks.

Sample answer 2

Schubert's *Der Doppelgänger* is a German lied, Romantic in style, while *Symphony of Psalms*, composed just over a 100 years later, is typical of Stravinsky's middle-period style. ◄── Good context.

Schubert's word-setting matches the stresses of Heine's poem with the musical stresses [1]. It is mainly syllabic [1], with only one extended melisma [1] near the end.

Stravinsky's setting is also syllabic for the most part [1], but he often displaces accents [1], e.g. when he moves the six-note phrase 'Laudate Dominum' to different parts of the bar. Stravinsky also breaks words up into their separate syllables, almost undermining the meaning of the text [1].

Schubert's melodic writing is declamatory, with short phrases separated by rests [1]. He can do this because the piano ostinato results in continuity. ◄── Irrelevant.

The melody is narrow in range at first, but gradually climbs higher for the two climaxes [1], and it is here that Schubert introduces typical chromatic harmony, in particular the German 6th chords. The pervading gloomy atmosphere is only alleviated at the end with the plagal cadence and tierce de Picardie. ◄── All the observations regarding harmony are irrelevant.

Stravinsky set out to praise God, but treats the text in an unusual way, avoiding obvious word-painting [1]. The whole of the last section, which mentions cymbals, is slow and soft [1 for location].

The melody in Stravinsky's piece is mainly modal (see the opening section which is in the Aeolian mode) [1]. Its chant-like repetitions [1] and relatively narrow ranges [1] show that he was influenced by Russian church music. Other sections have much wider intervals [1], e.g. the passage after the second fast passage with dotted rhythms [1 for location]. Other ideas are built on repeated notes [1].

Schubert also has the occasional leap [1], but not so many.

Examiner's points

This answer would achieve a mark of 17/18. There is some effective writing, particularly in the early stages. Towards the end there is a tendency to digress. The response ends with an afterthought rather than a conclusion.

Exercise

Suggest a brief concluding summary.

Sample answer 3

Mark this answer yourself, commenting at the end on its good points, but also mentioning ways in which it could have been improved. Check your assessment against the examiner's comments that follow, after completing your marking.

Schubert's song is really a ghost story set to music. Its spooky atmosphere is evident from the start in the deep piano part, with chords missing 3rds. Above this, the singer sets the scene: 'The night is calm, the streets are still, in that house my love lived'. Schubert sets these words in short phrases, divided by rests and piano interludes with poignant false relations. Sometimes the melody is intensified by appoggiaturas. The stillness of the night is suggested by the slow moving chords on the piano, and the repeated F♯ pedal. The vocal line also keeps sticking on F♯ to start with, though the line broadens to take in a descending tonic triad – a B minor chord.

In contrast, Stravinsky's *Symphony of Psalms* glorifies God, and uses a modified symphony orchestra as well as a four-part chorus. He deliberately goes in the opposite direction in his text-setting. There are no cymbals and loud music. It is uncertain what key the piece is in. Although it finishes on a bright C major chord, the opening appears to use C Aeolian minor, with some confusion with C major producing false relations.

Schubert's song is through-composed, but he keeps to the verse scheme of Heine's original poem. The voice moves higher for the climax – when the poet sees his own double. Here the pedal note stops and Schubert introduces a German 6th chord.

Stravinsky's middle passage is fast with prominent triplets representing Elijah's chariot. The other important motif is the one consisting of six quavers, all on the same note. This memorable idea is used for 'Laudate Dominum', sung syllabically. Stravinsky also makes the singers separate the syllables with rests, like the medieval hocket or hiccup.

| | Schubert finally goes on to finish by setting the question to the double. 'Why do you ape the pain of my love?' The music moves into D♯ minor with a chromatic rising bass before falling back into the home key, the memory of old pains emphasised by the melisma. There is a final sense of calm as the song closes on B major. |
| | There is also repose in Stravinsky after the excitement of the previous passage. This is the section with the famous ostinato, while the voices keep moving around E♭ with chromatic notes in a narrow range. After a few more 'Laudates', the piece closes on the C major chord. |

Examiner's points

The candidate made 15 valid points:
- Short phrases, divided by rests
- Appoggiaturas, persistent F♯, triadic shape
- (B) minor
- (C) Aeolian
- Voice moves higher for climax
- Six-quaver motif on same note
- Syllabic, hocket and melisma
- Ostinato, chromatic notes and narrow range.

However, there were a number of digressions, such as the chromatic bass, pedal note and German 6th comments. The response was also weakened by the step-by-step comparing and contrasting. This is rarely the best way to deal with such questions, as divisions in the music are artificially imposed and impede the presentation of the facts. It is generally better to deal with one work at a time. The fact that the response contains consideration of both works is enough to satisfy the 'compare and contrast' request in the exam.

Exercise

Draw up a plan for this answer, showing how observations might have been presented more efficiently.

SAMPLE QUESTION 4

Compare and contrast structure and texture in Weelkes' *Sing we at pleasure* **and Howlin' Wolf's** *I'm leavin' you***. (18)**

Before reading any further, attempt the question yourself. You will find it useful to compare your own answer against the mark scheme (indicative content) and sample answers that follow.

Indicative content	
Structure	**Weelkes**: binary, with repeats, and fa-la refrains; G major, with modal inflections, and brief modulations of no structural significance.
	Howlin' Wolf: strophic; 12-bar blues, in G, but using a minor pentatonic scale; introduction and fade.
Texture	**Weelkes**: five-part counterpoint, with imitation at various distances, e.g. 1 beat, 2 bars; some brief homophony.
	Howlin' Wolf: mainly melody-dominated homophony; stop time; monophonic introduction; dialogue between voice and guitar; double- and triple-stopped chords in lead guitar; two- and three-note chords in harmonica.

Sample answer 1

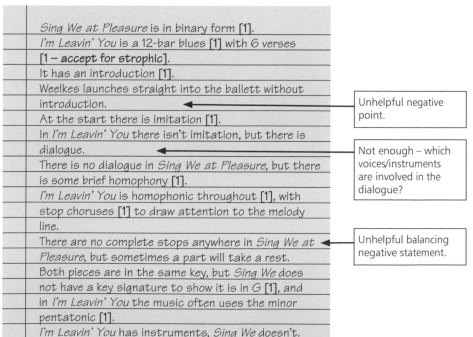

Sing We at Pleasure is in binary form [1].

I'm Leavin' You is a 12-bar blues [1] with 6 verses [1 – accept for strophic].

It has an introduction [1].

Weelkes launches straight into the ballett without introduction. ← Unhelpful negative point.

At the start there is imitation [1].

In *I'm Leavin' You* there isn't imitation, but there is dialogue. ← Not enough – which voices/instruments are involved in the dialogue?

There is no dialogue in *Sing We at Pleasure*, but there is some brief homophony [1].

I'm Leavin' You is homophonic throughout [1], with stop choruses [1] to draw attention to the melody line.

There are no complete stops anywhere in *Sing We at Pleasure*, but sometimes a part will take a rest. ← Unhelpful balancing negative statement.

Both pieces are in the same key, but *Sing We* does not have a key signature to show it is in G [1], and in *I'm Leavin' You* the music often uses the minor pentatonic [1].

I'm Leavin' You has instruments, *Sing We* doesn't.

Examiner's points

This response would gain 10/18. The candidate wrote in coherent complete sentences, but clearly lurched from one work to another, one observation triggering a not always relevant or positive remark about the other piece. It was not always very clear which work was being discussed.

> ## Exercise
>
> Boost the candidate's mark by cutting out the irrelevant passages and grouping sentences together in paragraphs, supplementing points whenever possible (perhaps regarding structure in the Weelkes). Provide brief introductory and concluding remarks.

Sample answer 2

	Weelkes	Howlin' Wolf
Structure	Binary form [1], with repeats [1] and refrains	
		In G major [1] with pentatonic minor blues scale [1]
Texture	5-part counterpoint [1]	
		Stop choruses [1]
	Some homophony [1]	
		Rhythm and blues ◄——— Irrelevant.

Examiner's points

This answer would gain 7/18.

> ## Exercise
>
> Complete the empty spaces where appropriate with a corresponding point about the other work. If you think you can only write a negative comment (for example, 'it is not contrapuntal'), leave the gap blank.

Sample answer 3

Mark this answer yourself, commenting at the end on its good points, but also mentioning ways in which it could have been improved. Check your assessment against the examiner's comments that follow, after completing your marking.

> There are huge differences between the English Renaissance ballett and the Chicago-style rhythm and blues number. For a start, the Weelkes is for unaccompanied voices and is clearly cheerful, while *I'm leavin' you* is for a relatively large band, and is distinctly gloomy.
>
> Weelkes has two sections, both repeated, and always ending with fa-la refrains. *I'm leavin' you*, however, is a 12-bar blues with several verses, introduction and fade.
>
> Although *Sing we at pleasure* was written before the establishment of major-minor tonality, it is obviously in G. The occasional F♮ makes it seem in the Mixolydian mode. The C♯ propels the music into the dominant, but modulations are so short-lived they have no effect on the structure.
>
> *I'm leavin' you* is in G, but the instruments are instructed to use G minor pentatonic giving a more bluesy feel. Regarding texture, *Sing we* is contrapuntal, with short chordal passages, e.g. 'Sweet love shall keep the ground'. There are many imitations, such as at the opening where the upper parts come in with the same melody, the second one copying the first after one bar.
>
> Howlin' Wolf's number is melody-dominated homophony throughout, apart from brief snatches of monophony in the intro. Variation is achieved by stop choruses, leaving the melody unaccompanied for a moment. There is also dialogue between the voice and guitar, and at one point harmonica and guitar – a passage involving some multiple stopping.
>
> In the end it seems there is almost no point of contact between the pastoral mood of Weelkes and the hard-edged blues of Howlin' Wolf – whether in musical techniques or the message conveyed.

Examiner's points

This answer was well written and organised, and made more than enough points to be awarded full marks.

Exercise

List any additional points the candidate could have made.

Revision notes 2015

Here we have provided a series of revision notes that will help you to focus on the most important aspects of each set work. It would be wise not to try to memorise everything for a parrot-like recitation of facts and figures. We suggest instead that you check you understand the main points, or generalisations, given under the various headings. After this, try to absorb some of the additional examples, which will often then help you to think of your own examples that can be used to illustrate the work in question.

It is important that you keep referring to the Edexcel Anthology, and associate the points made in the following pages with what you hear in the music and see in the score. Any attempt to learn these points in the form of abstract crib notes means you do not get anything out of the exercise in the long term, and run the risk of error in the exam.

INSTRUMENTAL MUSIC 2015

Bach – Brandenburg Concerto No. 4 in G: movement I

Background	• This work is one of the six Brandenburg concertos composed between 1717 and 1722. These concertos are so-called because Bach dedicated them to the margrave (ruler) of the state of Brandenburg. • The work is a concerto grosso – a type of concerto written for a group of soloists and orchestra. • The set work excerpt is the first of three movements (in a typical fast–slow–fast pattern). • Bach was strongly influenced by Vivaldi in his approach to the concerto grosso.
Rhythm and metre	• The movement is in a fast $\frac{3}{8}$ (Allegro). • There are almost continuous semiquavers (or demisemiquavers) throughout. Such steady, insistent rhythmic patterns are known as motor rhythms. • There is frequent syncopation. • There are occasional hemiolas (e.g. bars 80–81).
Melody	• The melody largely consists of broken-chord patterns and scalic figures. • Short motifs are spun out into longer melodic lines, through sequence, inversion, varied repetition, and various rhythmic and melodic elaborations. This is known as *fortspinnung*.

Harmony	• The harmony is functional and mainly diatonic; most of the chords are root-position or first-inversion triads.
	
	 • There is a varied harmonic rhythm, which often speeds up towards cadences and slows down in the solos.
	
	 • Harmonic features include:
	
	   • Dominant 7ths
	
	   • A Neapolitan 6th in bar 151 when the music moves to a minor key
	
	   • Frequent harmonic sequences
	
	   • Half-diminished chords
	
	   • A circle of 5ths in bars 97–103 when the music modulates from G to D major
	
	   • Pedal notes
	
	   • Suspensions.

Structure and tonality	• The movement is in ritornello form, in G major. • Modulations mark the different stages of the structure. • The main sections are as follows:

Theme	Key
Ritornello	G major
Episode	
Ritornello	E minor
Episode	
Ritornello	C major
Episode	
Ritornello	B minor
Opening ritornello	G major

• The middle ritornelli always end with the equivalent of the last 15 bars of the opening ritornello.

Resources and texture	• The instrumentation is typical for a Baroque concerto grosso: there is a concertino (solo group) of two recorders and violin, plus a strings ripieno section with harpsichord continuo.
	• The texture is best described as melody-dominated homophony.
	• However, there is also some counterpoint including brief snatches of imitation/canon.
	• There are some short passages with a three-part texture, as you would find in a trio sonata.
	• After the opening ritornello there is a passage for solo violin, accompanied by intermittent chords.
	• The recorders often play in parallel 3rds or 6ths (e.g. bars 66–75).
	• The violin has the most demanding solo part, with:
	• A wide range, from open-string G to the G three octaves above
	• The use of fifth position
	• A rapid demisemiquaver passage from bar 187
	• Double- and triple-stopping.

Shostakovich – String Quartet No. 8, Op. 110: movement I

Background	• Composed in 1960 following the composer's enforced membership of the Communist party in Russia, and a visit to Dresden where it was still possible to observe the effects of bombing during World War II. The work was dedicated to the 'memory of the victims of fascism and war'.
	• The quartet is autobiographical, with extensive use of the motif D–E♭–C–B, a musical cipher which stands for an abbreviated form of the composer's name (DSCH in German, or D(mitri) Sch(ostakovich)), as well as quotations from some of his earlier works.
Rhythm and metre	• The movement is in slow (Largo) simple quadruple time ($\frac{4}{4}$) throughout.
	• Shostakovich uses no note values shorter than a quaver, and many very much longer.
	• There are a few dotted rhythms.

Melody	• The melody is primarily in a low tessitura.
	• Phrases are often chromatic.
	• Prominence is given to the DSCH motif.
	• Some melodic material is taken from earlier works (e.g. Symphony No. 1 at bar 19).
	• Melodies also feature:
	• Appoggiaturas (e.g. bar 30)
	• Conjunct movement (e.g. from bar 55)
	• Some narrow-range motifs (bars 59–60 in violin II)
	• Repetitive figures (e.g. bars 50–56 in the violins)
	• Sequence (e.g. bars 19–23 in the viola).
Harmony	• There are some clearly defined, traditional progressions (e.g. a perfect cadence at bar 26, with a suspension, preceded by V–Ib–IV):
	• There are also some less traditional chord progressions (e.g. bars 79–81 consist of G major, E♭ minor, F major, with chromatic inner parts).
	• In addition, there are passages of harmonic stasis (i.e. no progression as such), e.g. the drone at bar 28 or tonic pedal on C at bar 50.
Structure and tonality	• The music unfolds without reference to traditional forms, although the movement could be described as having an arch shape: ABCB¹A¹.
	• At the start of the movement the tonality seems ambiguous, due to the chromaticism.
	• Tonic and dominant pedal notes help to reinforce the tonality once the key of C minor has been established.
Texture	• Shostakovich draws on a variety of textures, such as:
	• Four-part imitation (bars 1–11)
	• Two-part counterpoint (bars 19–22)
	• Homophony (bars 23–27)
	• Drone with melody in violin I (bars 28–44)
	• Four-part free counterpoint (bars 92–94)
	• Brief monophony (e.g. bar 124)

Poulenc – Sonata for Horn, Trumpet and Trombone: movement I

Background	• This work was composed in 1922.
	• Poulenc adopts a witty, irreverent, Neoclassical style, showing influences of Stravinsky.
	• This excerpt is the first movement of a three-movement work.
	• It is intended for concert performance by professional players.
Rhythm and metre	• The movement is in simple quadruple time ($\frac{4}{4}$), with occasional $\frac{3}{4}$ bars.
	• The tempo changes fairly frequently (e.g. the central section consists of a slow passage – *Plus lent* – followed by a faster one – *Plus vite*).
	• Other features include:
	• Syncopation (e.g. bars 9–17)
	• Anacrusis (e.g. the opening trumpet melody)
	• Augmentation (e.g. the opening motif is augmented in bars 22–25, into quavers and crotchets).
Melody	• The melody is largely diatonic.
	• Periodic phrasing reflects the Neoclassical influence (e.g. bars 1–4 and 5–8).
	• The work opens with a broken-chord motif, which is later modified (e.g. at bar 40).
	• There are two-octave leaps in the trumpet part in bars 36–38.
	• There is some ornamentation, e.g. the grace notes in bars 10 and 12.
Harmony	• Poulenc uses functional progressions with cadences (a result of the Neoclassical influence).
	• However, dissonances often cloud the harmony (e.g. in bar 4, a dissonant C in the horn part is introduced into a traditional Ic–V–I cadence).
Structure and tonality	• The movement is in a modified ternary form, with a short coda:

A	G major (modulating to D major and back)
B	In two parts: *Plus lent* (E♭ major) and *Plus vite* (B♭ major)
A¹	Modified repeat of section A, incorporating material from section B (G major)
Coda	4-bar coda in G major (although initially clouded by chromaticism)

Resources	• The work is written for:
	• Horn in F (sounding a 5th lower than written)
	• Trumpet in C (non-transposing)
	• Trombone.
	• All parts require considerable skill in performance.

Texture	• The texture mainly consists of melody-dominated homophony.
	• There are brief snatches of monophony (e.g. bars 26–27) and homophony (e.g. the final bar).
	• The limited instrumentation enables only lean harmonic support, so broken-chord patterns are sometimes used to supply this element (e.g. horn at the start of the *Plus lent* section).
	• At bar 40 there is an 'om-pah' accompaniment split between trumpet and trombone.

Mozart – Piano Sonata in B♭, K. 333: movement I

Background	• This work was composed in 1783.
	• It was intended as much for domestic or instructional purposes as for concert use.
	• The set-work excerpt is the first movement of a Classical three-movement sonata.
Rhythm and metre	• The movement is in simple quadruple (common) time.
	• The first subject starts with an anacrusis.
	• There is occasional syncopation (e.g. bar 5).
	• Runs of semiquavers are common, particularly towards the end of the second subject.
Melody	• There is some typically Classical periodic phrasing, e.g. at the start of the second subject.
	• In contrast, the first subject consists of a four-bar phrase that is followed by a six-bar answer.
	• Chromatic inflections are frequent.
	• Melodies are often extended by the use of sequence, e.g. in the second subject:
	• Ornamentation includes appoggiaturas (both diatonic and chromatic), turns and trills.
Harmony	• The harmony is functional, with regular cadences to define keys.
	• Mozart uses the typically Classical cadential $^6_4$ (Ic–V$^{(7)}$–I), e.g. in bars 57–59.
	• Most of the chords are root-position or first-inversion triads, although there is some chromatic harmony, including:
	• Appoggiatura chords
	• Diminished 7th chords
	• Augmented 6th chords.

Structure and tonality	• The movement is in sonata form, with three main sections:

Exposition	Short first subject in B♭ major, linking with a transition to a longer second subject in F major.
Development	Passes through a range of keys including C minor and G minor.
Recapitulation	Returns to the exposition material but now just in B♭ major.

Resources and texture	• This work would have originally been played on an early wooden-frame piano (known today as a fortepiano). This had a more delicate sound and narrower range than the modern piano. But unlike the harpsichord, it was able to create dynamic contrasts.
	• The texture is best described as melody-dominated homophony. The right hand carries the melody throughout.
	• The texture often consists of only two lines. The left-hand frequently uses a broken-chord accompaniment, or occasionally an Alberti bass.
	• Fuller chords are sometimes used, such as at the start of the second subject.
	• Very occasionally the right-hand plays octaves.

Alberti bass is a particular form of broken-chord accompaniment in which the figuration consists of a recurring four-note pattern in the order low-high-middle-high:

VOCAL MUSIC 2015

Tavener – The Lamb

Background	• This work was composed in 1982.
	• It is a setting of a poem by William Blake.
	• Although non-liturgical, it is sometimes sung as an anthem in the Anglican service of Evensong. It is also a popular work in carol services at Christmas.
Rhythm and metre	• There is no time signature or regular pulse.
	• The performance direction reads 'flexible – always guided by the words'.
	• The work consists mainly of even quavers, with some longer note lengths to mark the end of each phrase. It is primarily homorhythmic.
	• Augmentation is applied at the end of each verse.

Melody and word setting	• The word setting is mainly syllabic, with occasional slurs.
	• The three upper vocal parts have a narrow range, e.g. an augmented 5th (E♭–B♮) in the soprano part.
	• The bass part covers a wider range of a 12th (E–B).
	• The opening motif generates material for the whole piece, and consists of four pitches that circle around the note G (G–B–A–F♯).
	• The remaining melodic material is derived from either repetition (e.g. bar 3) or retrograde (e.g. bar 4) of the original phrase.
Harmony and tonality	• Different phrases of the work could be described as tonal, bitonal or modal, e.g.:
	• The first bar suggests G major.
	• The second bar is bitonal: the sopranos stay in G major but the alto line suggests E♭ major (it is an inversion of the soprano line).
	• The final bar is in the Aeolian mode on E.
	• Some of the harmonic writing seems quite conventional, e.g.:
	• The four-part harmony based on triads and 7th chords.
	• The double suspensions in bars 7–10, which are prepared and resolved.
	• Other aspects are less conventional, e.g. consecutive 5ths in the soprano and tenor parts.
Structure	• The work is strophic.
	• There are two verses; the second is essentially the same as the first but has a fuller texture.
Resources and texture	• The work is written for four-part unaccompanied choir (SATB).
	• The dynamic range is restricted to *mp*–*pp*.
	• Various textures are employed:
	• Monophony (e.g. bar 1)
	• Two-part homophony (e.g. bar 2)
	• Four-part homophony (e.g. bars 9–10)
	• Octaves (e.g. bar 11)
	• Octave pairings of soprano and tenor, alto and bass (e.g. bars 15–16).

Monteverdi – Ohimè, se tanto amate

Background	• This work is a madrigal (a secular work for a group of solo voices, in this case unaccompanied).
	• It is a setting of a text by the poet Guarini.
	• The work was published in 1603.
	• Though still unaccompanied, this madrigal shows many signs that Monteverdi was writing in a newer, more modern style (stile rappresentativo/representational style or seconda practica/second practice), as opposed to the older Renaissance style.
	• Because of the complexity of the writing, this madrigal was probably intended for trained singers rather than amateurs.
Rhythm and metre	• The work is in simple quadruple time.
	• Monteverdi attempted to reproduce the inflections of Italian speech in the music, and as a result there is considerable variety in the rhythmic patterns.
	• Some passages simply consist of steady crotchets (e.g. bars 47–51), while others are much more varied.
Melody and word setting	• The word setting is mainly syllabic.
	• Music is subordinate to the text (i.e. the purpose of the music is to express the text as clearly as possible).
	• Accented syllables usually appear on a strong beat, while unaccented syllables tend to appear on a weak beat.
	• Repeated notes are often used to aid clarity of the text.
	• Much of the melody is made up of conjunct movement or small leaps. Any larger leaps are often followed by stepwise movement in the opposite direction (e.g. soprano part bars 8–9).
	• There is some use of sequence, e.g. the last 20 bars.
	• Notice the sigh-like falling 3rd used for 'ohimè'.
	• The new style is evident in the use of intervals which had previously been avoided, e.g. the tritone.

Harmony and tonality	• Monteverdi's harmony primarily consists of root-position and first-inversion triads.
	• However, there are also many dissonances (often unprepared).
	• Typical features include:
	• False relations (e.g. B♭ against B♮ in bar 49)
	• Tierce de Picardies (e.g. bars 38–39)
	• Tonic and dominant pedals (e.g. bass part bars 61–65)
	• IIIb–I final cadence.
	• The work predates the functional harmony developed in the Baroque period, but can be described as being in G minor, with sections in D minor and B♭ major. Note the 'modal' key signature with only one flat.
Structure	• The work is through-composed, with each section of the text being treated separately.
	• However, the falling 'ohimè' recurs frequently, and so provides a unifying element.
Resources and texture	• The work is written for five unaccompanied voices, the canto and quinto corresponding to two soprano parts.
	• A variety of textures are employed to help convey the sense of the poem, e.g:
	• Paired alto and tenor in dialogue with paired canto and quinto over a sustained bass
	• Homophony for three voices in various groupings
	• Homophony for five voices
	• Some limited imitation
	• Free counterpoint.

Fauré – Après un rêve

Background	• This work is a *mélodie* (a French art song of the Romantic period). It was published in 1878 as part of a collection of three songs for voice and piano.
	• *Après un rêve* ('After a dream') tells of a longing to return to lost dreams of love.
	• The modest vocal range of an 11th, with no extremely high or low notes, makes the song suitable for amateur performers, as does the relatively simple piano part.
	• Songs like this would have been performed in the home, or to small gatherings in the fashionable salons of Paris and other cities.

Rhythm and metre	• The time signature of $\frac{3}{4}$ is a simple triple metre and the tempo marking of *Andantino* suggests a moderate, relaxed speed.
	• The piano accompaniment consists of a pulsating rhythm of continuous quavers in the right hand, supported by a sustained bass part in the left.
	• The voice part has much more varied rhythms, with triplets, dotted and tied notes reflecting the fluidity of the French language.
	• Triplet quavers in the vocal part create cross rhythms against even quavers in the accompaniment.
Melody and word setting	• The melody is entirely in the vocal part, and is not shared by the accompaniment.
	• The phrases are long and continuous, with only one rest for the singer (between the first two verses).
	• The melody combines stepwise movement with expressive leaps.
	• Many of the phrases are arch-shaped, but the last verse descends from a climactic top note to end on the lowest note of the song.
	• The word setting is mainly syllabic, but melismas are used to express important words.
Harmony and tonality	• Chord progressions are functional with cadences.
	• Much of the harmony is chromatic and many chords include 7ths and 9ths.
	• There are false relations between the voice and piano (e.g. B♭ against B♮ in bar 7). These give a modal feel to the vocal line.
	• The first 9 bars are based on a circle of 5ths.
	• The work is in C minor, with brief modulations to the relative major (E♭ major) and in the subdominant direction (F minor and B♭ minor).
Structure	• The work has a modified strophic form: similar music for the first two verses, but the third is different (to reflect the poet's awakening from the dream).
Resources and texture	• The work is written for solo soprano with piano accompaniment.
	• The texture is melody-dominated homophony throughout. All of the melodic material is in the voice part, and the piano provides a purely chordal accompaniment (with repeated quaver chords in the right hand, and mostly octaves in the left hand).

The Kinks – Waterloo Sunset

Background	• This rock ballad by singer-songwriter Ray Davies (leader of The Kinks) was released in 1967.
	• It captures a uniquely English flavour with its narrative of mundane London life, and its avoidance of American influence in both the music and the lyrics – factors that would later make the song influential in the Britpop style of the 1990s.
Rhythm and metre	• The time signature of **C** is a simple quadruple metre, and the song is recorded at an unhurried, moderate tempo.
	• A crotchet pulse, sometimes elaborated with quavers, is maintained by the accompaniment.
	• In contrast, the main vocal phrases tend to begin halfway through the bar and feature syncopation.
	• A repeating pattern of quaver and two semiquavers, first heard in the introduction, appears in several sections, sometimes in a modified form.
Melody and word setting	• The word setting is entirely syllabic.
	• The song is based on a five-note hook, repeated in a descending sequence, with suspensions created by the syncopations:
	• This phrase ('A') forms the basis of each verse, and is also heard in the intro and outro. The melody (but not the harmony) of this phrase uses the major pentatonic scale on E (E–F♯–G♯–B–C♯).
	• Phrase A begins and ends on the submediant (C♯) – a relatively weak note that is not part of the tonic chord.
	• The melody of the middle eight is basically a five-note scale that descends to end on the dominant, which is then repeated in a varied form (with an ascending octave leap).

Harmony and tonality	• The song is in E major throughout. Chords outside this key are C♯ in phrase B (see 'Structure' below) and F♯ in the middle eight, but these are secondary dominants that add chromatic colour rather than heralding modulations to new keys.
	• Phrase A is harmonised with chords I, IV and V^7. Their effect is softened by the use of first inversions.
	• Inverted chords also feature in phrase B, which centres on chord II (F♯m) and its dominant (C♯).
	• The middle eight focuses on dominant harmony (B and its dominant F♯).
	• In most of the song, the harmonies change no faster than one chord per bar.
	• The outro forms a mirror image of the intro. The intro starts with repetitions of the dominant 7th, followed by phrase A, while the outro starts with a statement of phrase A and then fades out on repetitions of the dominant 7th.
Structure	• The song is strophic, with a contrasting middle eight:
	<table><tr><td>Intro</td></tr><tr><td>Verse 1</td></tr><tr><td>Middle eight + 2-bar turnaround</td></tr><tr><td>Verse 2</td></tr><tr><td>Middle eight + 2-bar turnaround</td></tr><tr><td>Verse 3</td></tr><tr><td>Instrumental (based on verse) and outro (coda) for fade out</td></tr></table>
	• Each verse is in 16-bar popular song form (four 4-bar phrases, in the pattern AABA).
	• Each middle eight consists of a 4-bar phrase that is immediately repeated.
Resources and texture	• The instrumentation includes: electric (lead) guitar; acoustic (rhythm) guitar; bass guitar and drums.
	• The solo vocal line is double-tracked to thicken the sound, and is sung by the composer of the song, Ray Davies, who also plays rhythm guitar.
	• Backing vocals are sung by the other two guitarists plus Davies' wife.
	• The lead guitar takes the solo in the intro and outro. During the verse it tends to play short licks in dialogue with the voice.

Texture	• The texture of the song is melody-dominated homophony.
	• A walking bass, formed by a descending scale in repeated quavers, underpins the intro.
	• Descending scale patterns in the bass feature in much of *Waterloo Sunset*. They are the cause of many of the inverted chords heard in the song.
	• In the middle eight, the bass shadows the falling scale in the vocal line to create a heterophonic texture.
	• Backing vocals mainly sustain the harmony, but briefly imitate the lead vocal at the end of the middle eight and in the final bars of the song.

Van Morrison – Tupelo Honey

Background	• This song was recorded in 1971.
	• Over 7 minutes in length, it is unusually long for a pop song.
	• The song shows the influences of soul (in the rhythmic freedom and fragmentary lines) and folk music (in the pentatonic writing).
Rhythm and metre	• The song is in quadruple (common) time, with a slow tempo and laid-back feel.
	• Syncopation features heavily throughout the song.
	• Many of the vocal phrases start on an offbeat.
	• There are some cross rhythms (e.g. between the electric and acoustic guitars in bars 33–35).
Melody and word setting	• The vocal line is mainly syllabic, with occasional short melismas.
	• It is primarily based on improvised variations of the 2-bar melody played by the flute at the start of the introduction.
	• The vocal line is broken up into short phrases separated by rests.
	• It is based on a pentatonic scale (B♭–C–D–F–G).
Harmony and tonality	• The song is in B♭ major throughout (i.e. there are no modulations).
	• The harmonic rhythm is slow and regular.
	• The whole song is built around a four-chord ostinato of B♭–Dm–E♭–B♭, with occasional use of F (chord V).
	• The harmony is largely diatonic, with very occasional ornamental chromaticism.
Structure	• The song has a verse-and-chorus form. Aside from the verses and choruses, there are the following additional sections: an introduction, instrumental, middle eight and coda.

Resources and texture	• The texture is frequently contrapuntal, because of the web of improvised melody lines. The texture becomes increasingly busier, and the dynamics louder, towards the end of the song.
	• The lead guitar is primarily used as a melody instrument, mostly in the upper part of its range.
	• There is some dialogue between the lead and backing vocals, e.g. in verses 2, 3 and 4.
	• Dialogue can also be seen between the guitars and lead vocals during the verses.
	• Flute and saxophone provide additional melodic interest: flute plays the opening four-bar melody in the introduction (heard again during the coda); saxophone plays during the first half of the instrumental.
	• The piano and organ play sustained chords (with occasional short fills).
	• The bass guitar plays decorated versions of the same two-bar bass line throughout.
	• The drum kit provides a continuous quaver pulse and fills.

Familia Valera Miranda (Cuba) – Se quema la chumbambá

Background	• This is an example of *son*, a type of popular music from Cuba, often used to accompany dancing.
	• Son developed in the first half of the 20th century and combines elements of Spanish and African music. It was influential in the more recent development of salsa music.
	• *Se quema la chumbambá* was recorded in 1994 by a family of six Cuban musicians who specialise in the study and performance of traditional music from Cuba.
Rhythm and metre	• The time signature of ¢ indicates simple duple time – two minim beats per bar, rather than four crotchet beats.
	• The most important rhythmic element in son is the syncopated ostinato played by the claves: 
	• This rhythm is called 3:2 son clave because of its pattern of 3 notes followed by 2 notes.
	• Syncopation is also important in the cuatro and vocal lines. All of these parts are silent on the first beat of their main two-bar patterns.
	• More varied rhythms (including triplets) are heard during the long cuatro solo, which also relies heavily on syncopation.
	• A constant quaver pulse is played on the bongos.

Melody and word setting	• The entire vocal melody is based on the same two-bar phrase (with slight variations).
	• It consists of call and response between the solo singer (pregón) and chorus (coro).
	• The pregón melody has a narrow range of a minor 6th.
	• The word setting is entirely syllabic.
	• The improvised melody in the cuatro solo is much more varied, with a wider range, larger leaps and some chromaticism.
	• The cuatro riff is primarily formed from broken chords (which also feature in the solo).
Harmony and tonality	• The song is in G minor throughout (there are no modulations).
	• The functional harmony is based entirely on tonic and dominant 7th chords. It consists of a repeated chord pattern of Gm–D⁷–D⁷–Gm.
	• The bass often anticipates a change of chord by a crotchet, as in bar 5 ('anticipation bass' is a common feature of son and salsa music).
Structure	• The main instrumental riffs (ostinati) are announced in a 12-bar introduction.
	• These form the accompaniment to the strophic verses that follow, in a call-and-response style.
	• In the middle of these verses is a long solo for cuatro and bongos.
Resources and texture	• The song is performed by:
	• Pregón (solo voice) and two-part coro (chorus, actually sung by the instrumentalists)
	• Cuatro (a guitar-like instrument with four pairs of metal strings)
	• Double bass
	• Latin-American percussion (maracas, claves, and high and low bongo drums).
	• The texture consists of melody-dominated homophony, largely based on ostinati (riffs).

Sample questions 2015

Below you will find examples of the type of questions normally set in Section B of the exam. There are eight sample questions in total: two 10-mark questions and two 18-mark questions for the instrumental set works, and the same again for the vocal set works.

For each question, three sample answers are given: two that are marked already, as by an examiner, and one that you can mark for yourself. You should find that having a go at the questions yourself, and then comparing your answers to the ones given in this book, is an excellent way to revise for the exam, and will really help you to understand how to improve your marks.

INSTRUMENTAL MUSIC 2015

SAMPLE QUESTION 1

Describe the stylistic features of Bach's Brandenburg Concerto No. 4: movement I which show that it was written in the late Baroque era. (10)

Before reading any further, attempt the question yourself. You will find it useful to compare your own answer against the mark scheme (indicative content) and sample answers that follow.

Indicative content	
Resources	Harpsichord continuo; idiomatic violin writing; recorders; solo group (concertino) and supporting strings (ripieno), typical of the concerto grosso.
Structure	Ritornello form; ritornelli in different keys; separated by episodes.
Rhythm	Motor rhythms; hemiola.
Melody	Motivic; use of *fortspinnung*; sequences.
Harmony	Functional; circle of 5ths.
Tonality	Functional, with modulations to related keys.

Sample answer 1

The ten points I wish to make about the piece are as
follows:
1. Written for Margrave of Brandenburg when Bach
   was working in Cöthen.
2. Typical German style of grosso, mixing flutes
   into the solo group.
3. Earlier Italian concerto grosso (Corelli) used string
   trio for solo group.
4. Use of harpsichord [1] is typical of Baroque music.
5. Arpeggio type of theme heard throughout – as in bar 1.
6. Bach often develops his melody by using sequence [1].
7. Highly contrapuntal throughout.
8. Many demisemiquavers in solo violin.
9. Finishes in same key, with same themes as at start.
10. Keeps to same time signature throughout.

True, but irrelevant.

Not enough information.

True, but irrelevant.

True, but this in itself is typical not just of Baroque music.

Misleading as the texture is primarily melody-dominated homophony.

The last three points are all insignificant, as they do not show that the music was composed in the late Baroque era.

Examiner's points

This answer would gain two out of a possible ten marks. The problem here is a failure
to give sufficiently focused information. Most comments are either inconsequential
or too general in nature. It is perhaps inadvisable to limit yourself to ten observations,
as you cannot be sure what will be deemed creditworthy.

Exercise

Replace points three, eight, nine and ten with specific, relevant facts (as
mentioned in the mark scheme). Use appropriate terminology.

Sample answer 2

Bach is regarded as one of the most important late Baroque composers.
This work is one of a set of six written for the Margrave of Brandenburg
about 1720, now regarded as some of the finest examples of the Baroque
concerto grosso [1].
As such it uses ritornello form [1], with the ritornelli appearing in
various related keys [1], separated by episodes [1]. This sort of structure
only became possible with the rise of functional harmony and tonality
[1] towards the end of the Baroque period – as can also be seen in the
works of Vivaldi and Handel.

> The instrumentation is also typical of the Baroque era, with the use
> of continuo provided by harpsichord [1] and the solo instruments, the
> violin and recorders [1] in the concertino [1], while the remaining forces
> make up the ripieno [1].
> Many other aspects of the writing are also to be found in the
> Baroque era, e.g. the hemiolas [1] found at the end of each of the
> ritornelli [1 for location]. Another device is the circle of 5ths [1].

Examiner's points

This answer would gain 10/10. It is a very good answer, although the final
paragraph fizzles out into a list of small, unrelated points.

Exercise

Rewrite the final paragraph to give a more structured conclusion.

Sample answer 3

Mark this answer yourself, commenting at the end on its good points, but also
mentioning ways in which it could have been improved. Check your assessment
against the examiner's comments that follow, after completing your marking.

> A very long ritornello – 83 bars as opposed to the eight bars in
> Brandenburg No 2 – it has 4 motifs – bars 1-6, 13-14, 35-39 and 79-
> 83 – Bach develops by spinning and sequence – he also varies tonality
> by changing instrumentation from violin to flutes and back again –
> ritornello means little return – the piece works like a rondo with the main
> themes returning over and over again – there are episodes in between
> – sometimes Bach modulates – He opens with string chords from the
> whole orchestra – there is no figured bass so that must mean Bach did
> not need a harpsichord – there is so much going on he did not need to
> fill anything in – especially when the solo violin plays a lot of very rapid
> notes – there are many scales and arpeggios which make it sound quite
> mathematical – the opposite to Romantic music which is warm and
> emotional – another feature of Baroque music – probably intended for
> performance at court for people who knew about music and wouldn't get
> bored by it – not many players involved, just a few strings – difficult to
> play, there is no let up, exhausting for players and listeners – typically
> energetic.

Examiner's points

This answer would achieve 4/10 for picking up on ritornello, sequence,
episodes and modulation. Spinning is not close enough to *fortspinnung*. The

presentation is very poor. There is no organisation, the whole thing almost reading like an unpunctuated stream of consciousness. In view of the quality of writing, an examiner might well be inclined to award only three marks rather than four on grounds of a general lack of clarity.

Exercise

Rewrite the four correct points, and add at least one additional observation for each point, giving a location whenever possible.

SAMPLE QUESTION 2

Describe the features in Piano Sonata in B♭: movement I by Mozart which are characteristic of the Classical era. (10)

Before reading any further, attempt the question yourself. You will find it useful to compare your own answer against the mark scheme (indicative content) and sample answers that follow.

Indicative content	
Structure	Sonata form.
Harmony	Cadences; functional harmony and modulation; some chromatic harmony.
Melody	Some periodic phrasing; appoggiaturas and ornamentation.
Texture	Melody-dominated homophony; occasional Alberti bass.
Resources	Fortepiano, permitting dynamic contrasts.

Sample answer 1

Mozart's first movement is in sonata form [1]. It has an exposition, development and recapitulation. The first part of the movement, the exposition, contains a first subject, transition and second subject. This is followed by the development, which is as short or as long as the composer wants, passing through different keys and varying the themes introduced in the exposition, or else introducing new material. There then comes a recapitulation in which the first and second subjects are brought back. There may be a coda – by Beethoven's time this almost amounted to a second development – and there may also be a slow introduction.

This abstract description of sonata form – though correct – is unlikely to earn the candidate any more marks because it does not refer directly to features in the Mozart sonata, for example the keys used.

As a classical composer, Mozart wrote for an early type of piano [1 – accept for fortepiano] as opposed to the harpsichord which had been so popular in Baroque times. The textures are much simpler, with less counterpoint. Generally Mozart uses homophony [1], and as this was written for a keyboard instrument there are numerous instances of Alberti bass [1], evident right from the start.

> Incorrect. The accompaniment in the opening bars involves broken chords rather than an Alberti bass.

The other element of the piano which Mozart was able to use effectively was dynamic contrast [1]. This was impossible on the harpsichord – where changes of volume could only be obtained by coupling up ranks of strings. Mozart still used some ornamentation however [1].

To sum up then, the most important classical features are sonata form, use of piano, homophony and dynamic contrast.

Examiner's points

This answer would achieve 6/10. The candidate failed to focus directly on the question, but at least made a good attempt to round off the response.

Exercise

Rewrite the first paragraph, replacing the abstract description of sonata form with specific information about this movement by Mozart.

Sample answer 2

Mozart composed his Sonata in B♭ in 1783, so it is typical of the classical style.

> Unhelpful remark, because too vague and flowery.

The melody writing is typically graceful and often uses balanced phrases [1], as in the first subject.

> Incorrect (the first subject consists of a 4-bar phrase followed by a 6-bar answer).

Mozart's harmony is also clear with regular cadences [1] to mark the phrase structure and keys.

Textures are also clear with mostly melody and accompaniment [1]. He also uses antiphony between hands.

> Incorrect.

Sonata form is used here [1].

He frequently uses appoggiaturas [1] to make the melody more expressive, and these are sometimes chromatic [1]. He also uses chromatic chords [1], e.g. diminished 7ths [1 for example] and augmented 6ths [1 for example]. Alberti bass appears sometimes [1].

> Mozart modulates frequently [1], going to the dominant
> – F – for the second subject [1 for example], but when
> it comes back in the recapitulation, it is in the tonic
> [1 for example].
> There is no introduction. ◄——————

| Unhelpful negative statement. |

Examiner's points

This answer would be awarded 10/10 as the candidate made 13 creditworthy points. However, the presentation of ideas is rather disorderly, and the answer would have been even better if the points had been made in a more logical order.

Exercise

Group the points made into paragraphs (melody, harmony, texture, structure and tonality), and write a brief conclusion to the answer.

Sample answer 3

Mark this answer yourself, commenting at the end on its good points, but also mentioning ways in which it could have been improved. Check your assessment against the examiner's comments that follow, after completing your marking.

> Mozart's Sonata in Bb major is a typical product of the Classical era, showing many traces of 18th-century styles. In particular it was music that was intended to please, and is characterised by lightness and grace. Mozart's melodic writing contains much ornamentation, with trills and appoggiaturas. It is varied by use of different rhythms, opening with a mixture of quavers, semiquavers and longer notes.
>
> His harmony is also very varied, going from full chords to single notes, and sometimes no accompaniment at all. The writing is diatonic throughout, and often moves into different keys, shown by the accidentals which appear throughout.
>
> The change of key is typical of Classical musical structure, a sort of binary form developed by Baroque composers. The two sections of the movement are clearly shown by the double bar. Typically the second section is much longer, and contains quite different ideas.
>
> Finally the Sonata is written for the piano which really only became fashionable in the second half of the 18th century. Mozart himself was an expert pianist and wrote many concertos for himself to play. The piano was a more expressive instrument than the keyboards previously used which only had a limited tonal range.

Examiner's points

There are four points here, three of which had to do with ornamentation, the other one with change of key. There was some confusion, notably because harmony was understood to refer to accompaniment and so equated with texture. No credit was allowed for the unhelpful remarks on rhythm and for stating that the harmony was diatonic throughout. Nor were marks awarded for reference to the piano as this is given in the question. Reference would need to be made to the early piano or fortepiano, and the remarks about the piano being more expressive were not clear enough to earn a mark for dynamic contrast.

Exercise

Retain the few correct points and rewrite those statements that are wrong. Add enough information to bring the total mark to 10/10.

SAMPLE QUESTION 3

Compare and contrast melody and texture in Bach's Brandenburg Concerto No. 4: movement I and Shostakovich's String Quartet in C minor: movement I. (18)

Before reading any further, attempt the question yourself. You will find it useful to compare your own answer against the mark scheme (indicative content) and sample answers that follow.

Indicative content	
Melody	**Bach**: many broken-chord patterns and scalic lines; use of sequence; use of *fortspinnung*; motivic; mainly diatonic.
	Shostakovich: low tessitura; largely in a minor key; use of cipher; chromaticism; quotation from earlier works.
Texture	**Bach**: contrasts between concertino and ripieno; continuo; melody-dominated homophony; snatches of imitation; trio-sonata textures; solo violin line with intermittent chordal accompaniment; pedal notes; recorders often in 3rds and/or 6ths.
	Shostakovich: imitative opening; chordal passages; melody and drone; monophony.

Sample answer 1

	Bach	Shostakovich	
Melody	Arpeggiated [1].	Uses cipher of his own name DSCH [1] – German for D E♭ C B♮ [1].	Misleading, because the melody passes through both major and minor keys.
	Sequence used [1].		
	Major key.	Mainly minor key [1].	
	Modulation.		Irrelevant.
	Melody in flutes and solo violin.		This question requires information on the melody itself, not which instruments are playing it.
Texture	Contrapuntal.	Drones and pedals used [1].	Misleading as a dangerous over-generalisation; it's common to categorise Bach's music as 'contrapuntal' when much of it is not.
	Very busy.	Melody and accompaniment.	
	Can be very thick, or very thin when there is just a solo violin.	Also, thick and thin.	
	Contrast of full band and groups of solo instruments [1 – accept].	Some heterophony.	Incorrect.
	Typical concerto grosso.	Some antiphonal passages.	Incorrect.
	Baroque style.	Classical string quartet.	

Examiner's points

There were seven points made, but the lack of clarity and coherence as well as the irrelevant remarks would probably lead the examiner to deduct a mark, perhaps leading to a total of 6/18.

> ## Exercise
>
> Extract the creditworthy points and rewrite them in complete sentences to avoid ambiguity.

Sample answer 2

Bach was writing to impress the Margrave of Brandenburg, while Shostakovich was writing autobiographically. It is even thought that this might have been a musical suicide note as Shostakovich was depressed at being forced to join the Communist Party, and by seeing the destruction of Dresden.

The autobiographical elements of Shostakovich's piece are its main theme – the DSCH cipher [1]. Shostakovich's initials which when spelled out in musical notes according to the German system, result in D E♭ C B [1].

There are no quotes in Bach's Brandenburg Concerto. It is simply an abstract instrumental piece, in which design is the most important aspect. It is in ritornello form, with the main theme appearing in various keys. In between these appearances of the ritornello come the episodes, where Bach often allows the concertino instruments a more obvious solo role [1].

Uninformative negative statement.

In the quartet, there are no obvious solo roles. Even though it is a 20th-century piece, it is much less colourful than Bach's work, as Shostakovich has used the Classical string quartet, invented by Haydn, of two violins, viola and cello. Not only that, he writes low down in the instrumental ranges [1], and even uses the lowest open strings on occasion. The result is a very sombre sound which is perfectly suited to the message he was trying to convey.

Another unhelpful negative statement.

As I said earlier, Bach was not trying to get any message across, and this accounts for the mathematical patterns in the music. For example, the use of sequences [1], giving the listener the feeling they know where they are going next.

Bach's melodies are diatonic [1], but Shostakovich often uses chromatic lines [1], which make it difficult to know what key the music is in. He also uses a much wider range of textures than in the Brandenburg, for example he starts [1 for location] with a sort of fugal exposition, with all the instruments coming in with imitations [1] of the DSCH motif. This does not keep going for very long, however, and in the middle section of the movement [1 for location], he introduces melody and drone accompaniment [1], and also harmonises DSCH in block chords [1].

> Even though Bach was famous for his fugues, there is scarcely any fugal writing in this movement though it is mainly contrapuntal most of the time. The exceptions come with single line writing for solo violin with occasional chords [1]. The other exception is the trio-sonata style of writing for the two recorders and continuo [1] in one of the middle episodes.

Incorrect as the primary texture is actually melody-dominated homophony.

Examiner's points

This answer would gain 14/18. It is generally coherent, but is rather weak in organisation and certainly long-winded.

Exercise

Cut out the irrelevant remarks and organise the remaining points together so that the argument no longer zigzags from one work to the other. Provide a short conclusion.

Sample answer 3

Mark this answer yourself, commenting at the end on its good points, but also mentioning ways in which it could have been improved. Check your assessment against the examiner's comments that follow, after completing your marking.

> The two works under discussion differ radically in their approaches to melody and texture. Bach's concerto is a typical late Baroque piece, while Shostakovich's quartet is cast in a tonal idiom favoured by the Soviet authorities for whom the composer was obliged to write.
>
> Bach's melodic writing is largely diatonic, and includes both broken chord patterns (bars one to two) and conjunct lines (bars three to six). His melodic writing is largely motivic, and he extends lines through fortspinnung, i.e. the extension of a musical line through sequential repetition, for example.
>
> The quartet creates a gloomy impression from the start: its melodies are mainly in a minor key, and are constantly in relatively low registers. There is some chromaticism as well. The most distinctive elements of the melodic writing arise from the use of the DSCH cipher, Shostakovich's musical signature (D E♭ C B) and quotations from the first and fifth symphonies.
>
> Regarding texture, Bach's concerto follows Baroque methods, employing a harpsichord continuo to provide harmony and divides the band into two parts; the concertino of two recorders and solo violin and ripieno, made up of the remaining strings. Overall the movement is broadly homophonic, with some passages for solo violin and occasional

chords. Bach also uses the recorders in a more involved three-part texture, rather like that of trio sonatas, in some of the episodes.

Shostakovich uses imitation at the start. Shortly after he introduces a two-part passage in dialogue, chordal homophony and an extended passage for melody and drone.

The very different effects produced by these movements can be explained by obvious contrasts of tempo, contrasts of key (major and minor), but also in the way the later work is kept to a lower pitch range with much use of drone effects.

Examiner's points

This candidate made 25 creditworthy points and so would easily be awarded 18/18. Notice how the candidate managed to make a large number of points without writing too much; try to emulate this economical style of writing in your own answers.

Exercise

List the 25 points made by the candidate in the answer above. (Hint: three of the 25 marks have been awarded for giving specific locations. For example, 'broken-chord patterns' would gain 1 mark, and 'bars one to two' another mark; 'Shostakovich uses imitation' would gain 1 mark, and 'at the start' a second mark. Note that 'in some of the episodes' is not specific enough to gain a mark: which episodes, and whereabouts?)

SAMPLE QUESTION 4

Compare and contrast the structure and tonality of Mozart's Piano Sonata in B♭: movement I and Poulenc's Sonata for Horn, Trumpet and Trombone: movement I. (18)

Before reading any further, attempt the question yourself. You will find it useful to compare your own answer against the mark scheme (indicative content) and sample answers that follow.

Indicative content	
Structure	**Mozart**: sonata form. **Poulenc**: ternary form, but with some modifications: A – B in two contrasting sections – A including passages from the central section – coda.
Tonality	**Mozart**: functional; cadences; modulations, e.g. to F for the second subject; a wider range of keys in the development; in the recapitulation, the second subject remains in the tonic. **Poulenc**: cadences; functional; in G major; modulates to D, E♭ and B♭; chromaticism in the coda makes the tonality less clear.

Sample answer 1

Mozart	Poulenc
Sonata form [1]	Ternary form [1]
With first subject	Starts in G [1]
Transition	Middle section has two
Second subject	contrasting parts [1]
Development	Slower passage in E♭ [1]
Recapitulation	Faster one in B♭ [1]
First subject	Final section combines first
Transition	section with music from
Second subject	faster middle part [1]
First subject in B♭	Coda [1]
Second in F [1]	Chromaticism obscures key
Much longer, can be divided	at the end [1]
into several subsections [1]	
In recap, second sub stays	
in B♭ [1]	

> This abstract account of sonata form is unlikely to gain any additional marks.

> The key is already given in the title.

Examiner's points

Twelve creditworthy points are made here, but in a rather clumsy way.

Exercise

Rewrite the section on Mozart more efficiently, avoiding the abstract account of sonata form. In other words, refer specifically to keys in relation to particular subjects, and where possible give other factual information about the various sections, for example that the transition ends with an imperfect cadence.

Sample answer 2

Poulenc's work is Neoclassical and shares a surprising number of features with the sonata by Mozart. He belonged to a group of French composers known as 'Les Six' who tried to move away from Romantic styles by returning to the simpler melodies and harmonies of the Classical period. This classification can be seen in a comparison of the melody of the opening with some of the themes written by Haydn and Mozart – especially the way they all use broken chords and scales.

> The opening paragraph suffers from an excess of unnecessary information and misapplied terminology, such as 'classification'. 'Classicising' is the correct term here.

The classification process is evident mainly in the harmonies and modulation schemes. Poulenc uses cadences [1], notably the perfect at the end of the first phrase [1]. The fact that he uses four-bar phrases also refers back to the balanced phrases of Mozart and Haydn [1]. He also uses clear key schemes. He begins in G [1], then modulates to the dominant – D [1] – at the end of the second 4-bar phrase [1 for location]. He also makes great play of major-minor contrasts, with the middle part of the movement starting in C minor.

> A mark has been allowed here as the candidate is referring to phrase structure.

> Incorrect – the middle section starts in Eb major.

In Mozart, there are obviously plenty of cadences [1] as the Classical style is all to do with functional harmony and tonality [1]. There is a perfect cadence at the end of the first subject [1], while the transition section finishes with an imperfect cadence [1].

There is more of a difference in structure with Poulenc using a simpler ternary scheme [1]. The central part differs immediately in its use of a slower section [1].

Mozart uses sonata form [1], the important thing being that the recapitulation's second subject is in the tonic [1], whereas the exposition finished in the dominant [1]. The central development reworks exposition material in various keys [1], e.g. F minor [1 for example].

Examiner's points

Seventeen creditworthy points are made in this response. In view of the irrelevancies and incorrect statements, an examiner may be inclined to award a mark of 15–16 as the work is good, but not outstanding.

Exercise

Improve the opening paragraph, and provide a brief conclusion.

Sample answer 3

Mark this answer yourself, commenting at the end on its good points, but also mentioning ways in which it could have been improved. Check your assessment against the examiner's comments that follow, after completing your marking.

> Mozart's sonata is Classical and is in sonata form.
>
> Poulenc's sonata is Neoclassical and is in ternary form.
>
> Mozart uses functional harmony and tonality.
>
> Keys are clearly recognisable in Poulenc's sonata, but he sometimes modulates to unrelated keys.
>
> Mozart does not modulate to unrelated keys, using the dominant for the second subject.
>
> Poulenc starts in G and moves to D by bar eight. He starts the middle passage in E♭, then goes to B♭. When the main theme returns (it is in ternary form), he goes back to G after a linking passage in A♭.
>
> Mozart does not use linking passages so his structures are obviously much more sectional. You can see the seams showing, but Poulenc's joins are much more skilful.
>
> Poulenc's piece also shows how music progressed by the 20th century as the instruments are much more sophisticated and can do much more. Mozart only had an early piano, and pianists could not play as well in the 18th century.
>
> Poulenc's piece would therefore have been for professionals, probably playing at a proper concert, while Mozart's would just have been for pianists to practise at home to improve their skills, as nobody would want to hear them until the next century.

Examiner's points

There are 11 creditworthy points: sonata form; ternary form; functional harmony and tonality in the Mozart; Poulenc's use of unrelated keys; dominant for the second subject in the Mozart; keys given in the Poulenc, i.e. G, D and location, E♭, B♭, return to G, but not A♭.

It was a rather bitty approach to begin with, and the remarks near the end were not very illuminating.

Exercise

Improve this answer by grouping related ideas together, and replacing the remarks at the end with more relevant points.

VOCAL MUSIC 2015

SAMPLE QUESTION 1

Describe the stylistic features of Monteverdi's *Ohimè, se tanto amate* which indicate that this work was written in the early Baroque era. (10)

Before reading any further, attempt the question yourself. You will find it useful to compare your own answer against the mark scheme (indicative content) and sample answers that follow.

Indicative content	
Context	Seconda pratica/stile rappresentativo.
Word setting	Music is subordinate to the text; follows Italian speech rhythms; mainly syllabic; representation of a sigh in the falling 'ohimè'.
Rhythm	Marked contrasts in rhythmic patterns.
Melody	Free use of previously forbidden intervals, such as tritones and 7ths; chromaticism.
Harmony	Unusual final cadence (IIIb-I); false relations; unprepared dissonance.
Texture	Abrupt contrasts of vocal groupings and types of texture; generally designed to ensure audibility of the text (e.g. the homophonic passages).

Sample answer 1

Monteverdi starts the madrigal off in G minor, but finishes [1 for location] with a tierce de Picardie into G major by way of an unusual concluding cadence of mediant to tonic (IIIb – I) [1].
    There are some typical unprepared dissonances [1], e.g. the tritone of Bb to E in the opening series of ohimès [1]. There is also much chromaticism [1] as well. All these features are typical of early Baroque music.

Notice that the marks here are not for the tierce de Picardie, which was very frequently used in early music, but for the unusual cadence at the end.

Examiner's points

This answer, despite its brevity, would gain 5/10. The most obvious omission arises from the failure to comment on the basic approach to word setting in early Baroque music.

Exercise

Improve this answer by providing a brief introduction that explains how Monteverdi's word setting is characteristic of the early Baroque period.

Sample answer 2

- Use of tritones [1].
- Unprepared dissonances [1], such as Bb to E [1].
- Abrupt changes to new key, e.g. opening is in G minor, then suddenly moves to Bb [1 – accept].
- Abrupt and frequent changes in texture [1], e.g. antiphonal at start going to homophony [1 for example].
- Lack of clearly defined structure – completely through-composed, so much more difficult to follow. ◄ — This is not specifically an early Baroque feature.
- Completely functional tonal harmony with no sign of earlier modal system. ◄ — Incorrect.

Examiner's points

This answer would gain 6/10. The remarks about structure and tonality were either irrelevant or incorrect, and as in the previous answer the candidate neglected to mention anything about Monteverdi's word setting.

Exercise

Rewrite the answer in complete sentences, and add a further four or five points to ensure that the candidate would gain full marks.

Sample answer 3

Mark this answer yourself, commenting at the end on its good points, but also mentioning ways in which it could have been improved. Check your assessment against the examiner's comments that follow, after completing your marking.

The most important innovations in early Baroque music involved the introduction of continuo and concertato contrasts between voices and instruments. We cannot see these features here – you would need to turn to Monteverdi's opera L'Orfeo or the Vespers for these, but some characteristic signs of a new artistic attitude can be observed.

This madrigal is a typical example of seconda pratica, and was the type of work which deliberately went against the earlier Renaissance approach of having the music dominate the text. Here the music is second to the text which had to be set so that it could be clearly heard. The text setting also follows the patterns of Italian speech, and so the word setting is largely syllabic, while the textures are often homophonic. This contrasts markedly with Renaissance music which is often melismatic and polyphonic.

Other features involve the use of awkward intervals. In Renaissance music, leaps were never very large, and almost always the part came back within that leap. Here Monteverdi allows the voices to sing awkward intervals, such as 7ths and tritones, and does not always make the voice return inside the original interval. It all contributes to the listener's appreciation of the pain experienced by the singers.

Monteverdi also combines parts to form unexpected dissonances. He rejects suspensions, i.e. prepared dissonances in favour of sudden discord. Again this heightens our appreciation of the sufferings of the singers who fully expect to die.

Last, but not least, there are the sighs of despair – the rests inserted between the *ohimès* – which again underline the message of this music.

Examiner's points

Ten points are made here, with a bit of a struggle (seconda pratica, music second to the text, Italian speech rhythms, syllabic, homophonic, awkward intervals, 7ths, tritones, unprepared dissonances, and rests). The introduction could have been more relevant (i.e. specifically about this set work), and the answer would have benefited from a conclusion.

Exercise

Draw up a new plan for this answer, including introductory and concluding observations, and listing points and examples that could easily be introduced.

SAMPLE QUESTION 2

Describe the features in *Se quema la chumbambá* which are characteristic of Cuban son. (10)

Before reading any further, attempt the question yourself. You will find it useful to compare your own answer against the mark scheme (indicative content) and sample answers that follow.

Indicative content	
Context	Typically used as music for dancing; a combination of Spanish and African influences.
Rhythm and metre	Simple duple time; constant quaver pulse on the bongos; syncopation; 3:2 son clave; some triplets.
Melody	Strophic/repetitive; range of a minor 6th in the pregón; some chromaticism; broken chords.
Harmony and tonality	G minor; alternating tonic and dominant chords; no modulation.
Texture	Melody-dominated homophony; with call and response.
Resources	Plucked strings (cuatro and double bass); percussion; solo pregón; two-part coro.

Sample answer 1

- *Se quema* is a typical combination of Spanish melodic style and African percussion [1].
- The melody is in G minor [1] with narrow range – minor 6th in vocal part [1].
- The harmony is also limited, with just two chords throughout. ← Not enough information – what are the chords?
- Rhythm is the most complex element here, showing African elements.
- Constant quavers giving pulse on bongos [1].
- Syncopation in claves [1].

Examiner's points

This answer would achieve 5/10, providing a few mainly isolated points.

Exercise

Add three further points to the answer above about the instrumentation, texture and chords used in this work.

Sample answer 2

Se quema was intended as entertainment music [1] and has a repetitive [1] melody split between the solo pregón [1] and two-part coro [1] in a call and response [1] texture, pointing to African influences

Further African elements can be found in the rhythmic scheme, e.g. the 3:2 son clave rhythm [1], that is the three-note syncopated [1] pattern in the first bar, followed by the two-note figure in bar two. Apart from percussion [1], there is the plucked cuatro [1] and double bass [1], as well as vocal parts.

The melody and harmony are more European or Spanish in style. The music is in a functional [1] G minor [1], and only uses tonic and dominant chords [1]. The melody line only spans a minor 6th [1], though a wider range can be seen in the cuatro part.

It can therefore be seen that son, like much Caribbean music, is a combination of European and African styles [1].

An effective opening paragraph that has already gained the candidate 5 marks.

Examiner's points

The candidate made 15 creditworthy points and so would easily be awarded the maximum of 10/10. The answer was well organised and coherent, and the ideas were linked together effectively.

Exercise

List any points in the mark scheme that were not included in the answer above. Decide in which paragraph you would include them.

Sample answer 3

Mark this answer yourself, commenting at the end on its good points, but also mentioning ways in which it could have been improved. Check your assessment against the examiner's comments that follow, after completing your marking.

Se quema opens with an instrumental introduction which leads straight into the main part of the peice when the voice comes in. After a while, the voices drop out, and the cuatro has a long and difficult solo.

The rhythms in this solo are even more complicated than in the main part of the peice, where only the bongos provide a definite pulse marking the beat.

This music is extremely repetetive all the way through except for another passage in the middle which would have been included to add interest to the music. Otherwise it would have been rather boring.

It is not just it goes on a bit. Most of the stuff in the anthology goes on a bit, but at least the other stuff has a wider range and variety – except for *The Lamb* which has even less notes than *Se quema*. *The Lamb* is also very repetetive.

The chords are just Dm and G⁷, which also makes for a rather boring result after a while. When the coro comes in, it has the same sort of idea as the pregon, producing imitation.

The rest of it is all rather homorhythmic apart from the passages which are polyrhythmic.

Examiner's points

This answer would achieve three points, these being the mention of the cuatro, the bongos marking the beat, and the repetitive nature of the song. Errors included the two chords named and the incorrect use of the term imitation. The final paragraph was nonsensical. There were a number of spelling errors.

Exercise

Help the candidate out by correcting the spelling errors (there are two words spelled wrong in the answer), and by offering some more substantial points about the music.

SAMPLE QUESTION 3

Compare and contrast melody and rhythm in *The Lamb* by John Tavener and *Waterloo Sunset* by The Kinks. (18)

Before reading any further, attempt the question yourself. You will find it useful to compare your own answer against the mark scheme (indicative content) and sample answers that follow.

Indicative content	
Melody	**Tavener**: very narrow range; initially diatonic/major; subsequently chromatic; melody often repeated; otherwise extended through retrograde; largely syllabic (some slurs).
	The Kinks: five-note hook ('Dirty old river'); forms a descending sequence; entirely syllabic; middle eight is characterised by a descending stepwise line, and ascending octave leap.
Rhythm	**Tavener**: rhythms guided by the words; no time signature; uses a limited range of note lengths; homorhythmic; augmentation.
	The Kinks: quadruple time; syncopation; repeated quaver – two semiquavers pattern; half-bar anacrusis.

Sample answer 1

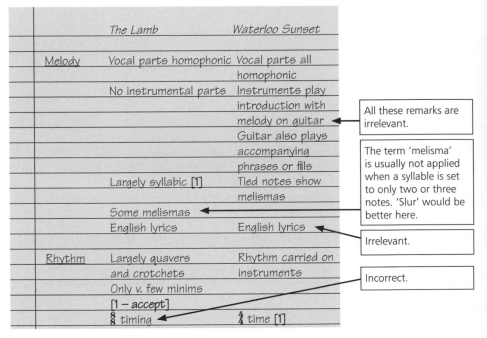

	The Lamb	Waterloo Sunset	
Melody	Vocal parts homophonic	Vocal parts all homophonic	
	No instrumental parts	Instruments play introduction with melody on guitar	All these remarks are irrelevant.
		Guitar also plays accompanying phrases or fills	
	Largely syllabic [1]	Tied notes show melismas	The term 'melisma' is usually not applied when a syllable is set to only two or three notes. 'Slur' would be better here.
	Some melismas		
	English lyrics	English lyrics	Irrelevant.
Rhythm	Largely quavers and crotchets	Rhythm carried on instruments	Incorrect.
	Only v. few minims [1 – accept]		
	$\frac{6}{8}$ timing	$\frac{4}{4}$ time [1]	

Examiner's points

The candidate could only be awarded 3/18 here. They were not focusing on the demands of the question, and misunderstood the correct use of the term 'melisma'.

Exercise

For each correct point made in the answer above, provide a correct balancing comment about the other work (for example, if *Waterloo Sunset* is in $\frac{4}{4}$, what is the time signature of *The Lamb*?) Then replace the irrelevant comments on texture and instrumentation with a couple of points for each work on melody and rhythm.

Sample answer 2

The melodic writing of *The Lamb* is mostly conjunct, unlike *Waterloo Sunset* which has the occasional octave leap [1]. *The Lamb* is almost all syllabic [1] with some melismas, or at least slurs covering two notes [1]. There are no slurs or melismas in *Waterloo Sunset*, as it is completely syllabic [1].

> Misleading.

> Needless negative statement.

The end of *The Lamb* [1 for location] is made to stand out by using rhythmic augmentation [1]. There is no exact rhythmic augmentation at the end of *Waterloo Sunset*, but there are longer notes there with suspensions lasting for several bars.

> Another negative statement and an error as well. Tied notes are frequently, and incorrectly, described as suspensions.

The Lamb uses monophony at the start, then the melody also appears in different parts, e.g. in octaves. *Waterloo Sunset* is melody-dominated homophony throughout.

> Irrelevant points about texture.

The Lamb uses a lot of serialist techniques to write the melody. The whole piece is made up from bar one in some way. Bar two alto is an inversion of bar one, bar six alto is a retrograde inversion of bar five soprano. Bar three soprano is made from the notes of bar one plus the alto's notes from bar two mixed in [1].

Bars 7 – 10 [1 for location] are a repeat of bar 1 [1]. In these bars the other parts are filling in the harmony. *Waterloo Sunset*, being pop music, does not use any of these serialist techniques. It just has an 'a' phrase and a 'b' phrase.

> A mark is only awarded for the final point, as the alto part here is a harmony rather than melody line.

The Lamb uses a lot of repetition, but *Waterloo Sunset* uses sequence [1] instead.

In *The Lamb*, dissonances are caused as a result of the melodic writing, e.g. bar two the F♯ against A♭. Dissonances are rarer in *Waterloo Sunset* – but there are the suspensions already mentioned.

> Incorrect.

Examiner's points

Ten points are made here, but as the quality of written communication is in need of improvement, and there is an evident lack of planning and a misunderstanding of terminology, the candidate would probably have been awarded only eight or nine marks.

> ## Exercise
>
> Remove the unhelpful negative remarks and irrelevant comments. Add another four or five correct points to bring the mark up.

Sample answer 3

Mark this answer yourself, commenting at the end on its good points, but also mentioning ways in which it could have been improved. Check your assessment against the examiner's comments that follow, after completing your marking.

Tavener	The Kinks
Words set to poem by William Blake	Lyrics are about 1960s film stars and London life
The Lamb represents both Jesus and childish innocence	
Mostly syllabic	Mostly syllabic
Use of melisma to stress important words	No melisma
Strophic, so melody repeated	Verse and middle eight
Conjunct	Some step movement
All music comes from bar one	Also octave leap
Bar one: tone row	
Bar two: alto inversion	Verse has aaba structure
Bar three: combines pitches of bars one and two	
Bar four: retrograde of bar three	Uses hook
No sequence	Sequence
Modal	Pentatonic
No time sig.	Strict $\frac{4}{4}$
Music drifts with the words	Syncopation
Antiphonal	Homophonic
Unaccompanied	Typical 1960s band with vocals and bvox
Performed in churches, though not really sacred	Performed at gigs and then recorded

Examiner's points

There are 13 creditworthy points in this answer:

For *The Lamb*:

- Mostly syllabic:
- Melody repeated
- Combined pitches in bar 3
- Retrograde in bar 4
- No time signature
- Music drifts with the words.

For *Waterloo Sunset*:

- Stepwise movement
- Octave leap
- Uses hook
- Sequence
- Pentatonic
- Strict $\frac{4}{4}$
- Syncopation.

However, the excessive irrelevance and lack of organisation would certainly lead to a reduction, perhaps to 12/18.

Exercise

Rewrite the answer above, retaining just the valid points and using complete sentences.

SAMPLE QUESTION 4

Compare and contrast tonality and texture in *Après un rêve* by Fauré and *Tupelo Honey* by Van Morrison. (18)

Before reading any further, attempt the question yourself. You will find it useful to compare your own answer against the mark scheme (indicative content) and sample answers that follow.

Indicative content	
Tonality	**Fauré**: C minor; functional progressions; cadences; circle of 5ths; modulations to related keys; modal elements; false relations.
	Morrison: B♭ major; no modulation; pentatonic elements in the melody.
Texture	**Fauré**: melody-dominated homophony; repeated chords in piano right hand; octaves in the left hand.
	Morrison: dialogue between guitars and lead vocals/backing and lead vocals; contrapuntal instrumental; cross rhythms; chordal support from piano.

Sample answer 1

Après un rêve	Tupelo Honey
This piece in a minor key throughout finishing with a perfect cadence [1] in C minor [1].	In B♭ major [1]. No change of key [1].
False relations [1] because of the modal elements [1].	No false relations, though the melody is pentatonic [1].
It is melody and accompaniment [1]. The accompaniment is on the piano.	It is melody and accompaniment. The accompaniment is for flute, saxophone, piano, drums etc.

Unhelpful negative.

Incorrect as *Tupelo Honey* is primarily contrapuntal.

This comment doesn't provide any information about the texture.

Examiner's points

There are eight observations here expressed in a very basic form.

Exercise

Rewrite the valid observations to form complete sentences.

Sample answer 2

- *Après un rêve* is minor [1]
- *Tupelo Honey* in major [1]
- *AuR* functional [1], with cadences [1] and modulations [1]
- *TH* has the same progression throughout, and so does not modulate [1]
- Aeolian mode vocal line in *AuR* [1]
- Pentatonic in *TH* [1]
- Chordal accomp. all the way through *AuR* [1]
- *TH* more contrapuntal [1]
- Verse + refrain in *TH*
- *AuR* 19th-century French song
- *TH* a slow rock ballad

The last three points are irrelevant.

Examiner's points

There are ten creditworthy observations here. The mark may be reduced because of the irrelevancies and poor quality of written communication.

> ### Exercise
>
> Improve the quality of written communication by rewriting the answer in complete sentences. Combine statements to make comparisons and contrasts more effective, such as 'Après un rêve is in a minor key, whereas Tupelo Honey is in a major one'.

Sample answer 3

Mark this answer yourself, commenting at the end on its good points, but also mentioning ways in which it could have been improved. Check your assessment against the examiner's comments that follow, after completing your marking.

Après un rêve is an example of a 19th-century French chanson and would of been performed in a concert hall. In contrast, Tupelo Honey is a popular ballad and was performed both live and in the recording studio.

In texture, there is no variety in Après un rêve, which is melody-dominated homophony throughout, the vocal line accompanied by the piano with a steady quaver rhythm throughout. The textures in Tupelo Honey are much more complicated, with sustained harmony in organ supporting the flute melody, which is decorated with additional guitar lines. When the voice enters, the accompaniment continues its complex rhythms, especially in the bass line. In the middle of the song, there is an instrumental section which is quite contrapuntal, with even more complicated rhythms (e.g. groups of four semiquavers against the triplet quavers). There is nothing as complicated as that in Après un rêve which only has triplets against groups of two quavers.

This means the composer can go in for a much more interesting tonal scheme as there is no textural distraction. The song is in C minor, but there are snatches of Aeolian mode in the vocal part.

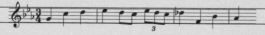

This results in false relations when B♭ sounds against the B♮ in the piano. False relation occurs when you get the same letter-name, but one of them is chromatically altered and comes either at the same time or on beats next to each other and in different parts as well. Another interesting feature is the circle of 5ths, clearly outlined in the bass part.

> The harmony and chord progressions are not so interesting in *Tupelo Honey* as he repeats the same thing throughout the song, which stays in B♭ throughout. There are several modulations in *Après un rêve*.
>   So the approaches are quite different, depending on the types of music and the audiences they were meant for.

Examiner's points

Hopefully you located 11 creditworthy observations. The quality of written communication was generally good, apart from 'would of' in the first sentence. There were a number of comments which did not quite hit the mark, such as the vocal line accompanied by piano with steady quavers which, though true, did not say anything about the textural aspect of the piece, while the example failed to illustrate the use of the Aeolian mode and in any case was highly approximate. The points which would have gained marks were: melody-dominated homophony throughout; sustained harmony (only just worth a mark, though – it was taken as an alternative for chordal); contrapuntal and fours against threes; minor, modal and false relations (notice that the long-winded definition of false relation here is unnecessary); circle of 5ths; B♭ throughout (two marks) and modulation in *Après un rêve*.

Exercise

List additional points the candidate could have made to earn full marks.

Glossary

This glossary is not comprehensive: it refers to terms as used in this volume. For more information about harmonic terms (e.g. suspension), see the AS Music Harmony Workbook and/or the A2 Music Harmony Workbook by Hugh Benham (Rhinegold Education, 2008). For fuller definitions of other terms and expressions, consult the Dictionary of Music in Sound by David Bowman (Rhinegold Education, 2002).

Added-note chord. Generally, an added-note chord includes a 2nd or 6th above the root in the bass; this 2nd or 6th forms part of the harmony and is not a non-chord note.

Aeolian mode. A scale that uses the following pattern of tones (T) and semitones (s): T–s–T–T–s–T–T. When starting on A, it consists of all the white notes within one octave on a keyboard.

Alberti bass. A particular type of **broken-chord** pattern often found in Classical keyboard music, with three pitches heard in the order low–high–middle–high (e.g. C–G–E–G).

Anacrusis. A note or notes preceding the first beat of a piece or phrase.

Antiphony. Performance by different singers/instrumentalists in alternation. Often – but not always – the different groups perform similar material.

Appoggiatura. A non-chord note that sounds on the beat and then resolves by step (up or down a semitone or tone) to the main chord note. The dissonant note is not 'prepared' as a **suspension** is. Although appoggiaturas are normally approached by leap, accented **passing notes** that are particularly long and/or prominent are often described as appoggiaturas, even though they are approached by step.

Arpeggio. A chord in which the notes are performed one after the other rather than at the same time. The adjective is 'arpeggiated'.

Atonal. Music that avoids keys or modes; that is, no pitch stands out consistently in the way the tonic does in tonal music.

Augmentation. The lengthening of the rhythmic values of a previously heard melody (e.g. where ♩♪♪ has become ♩♩♩).

Augmented interval. An augmented interval is one semitone larger than a major or perfect interval: for example, an augmented 4th (C–F♯) is one semitone larger than a perfect 4th (C–F).

Augmented 6th chord. A chromatic chord which in root position spans the interval of an augmented 6th, e.g. A♭–F♯. The chord also includes the major 3rd above the root (and sometimes also the perfect 5th or augmented 4th).

Backbeat. In pop and rock music, syncopated accents on the second and fourth beats of a 4/4 bar.

Ballett. A lighter type of **madrigal** (a form of secular vocal music cultivated in Italy and England in the 16th and early 17th centuries), with fa-la refrains and a generally **syllabic** setting.

Baroque. Refers to music written between about 1600 and 1750.

Binary form. A type of musical structure with two sections, each usually repeated (i.e. AABB).

Bitonal. Music that uses two different keys simultaneously.

Blue note. A note (usually the third, fifth or seventh degree of a major scale) performed at a slightly lower pitch than normal for expressive effect.

Britpop. A type of rock music that developed in Britain during the 1990s, strongly influenced by British pop music from the 1960s and 1970s. Important Britpop bands include Oasis and Blur.

Broken chord. A chord in which the notes are performed one after the other rather than at the same time.

Cadence. A pair of chords signifying the end of a phrase in tonal music. Cadences are of several types, of which perfect and imperfect are by far the most common. *See also* **Imperfect cadence, Interrupted cadence, Perfect cadence, Plagal cadence** and **Phrygian cadence**.

Cadential ⁶₄. Chord Ic preceding chord V or V⁷ in a perfect or imperfect cadence.

Call and response. A pair of phrases, usually performed by different musicians, in which the second phrase is heard as a reply to the first. Usually refers to jazz, pop and world music.

Canon. A strict form of **imitation**, often lasting for a substantial passage or entire piece, where the second part is an exact (or almost exact) copy of the first, even if at a different pitch.

Cantus firmus. An already existing melody (frequently a plainchant or chorale) to which other freely composed parts are added to make a new piece.

Chordal. A form of **homophony** in which all the parts move together in the same or very similar rhythm. The term homorhythmic (literally 'same rhythm') is sometimes used instead.

Chromatic. A chromatic note is one that does not belong to the scale of the key currently in use. For example, in D major the notes G♯ and C♮ are chromatic. The tonality of a passage containing many chromatic notes may be described as chromatic.

Circle of 5ths. A harmonic progression in which the roots of the chords move by descending 5ths (and/or ascending 4ths), for example B–E–A–D–G–C, etc.

Claves. A pair of short sticks that are used to play the clave rhythm in son and salsa music.

Coda. A concluding section of a movement.

Compound time. A metre in which the main beat is subdivided into three equal portions, as opposed to the two equal portions in **simple time**.

Concertino. The group of solo performers in a **concerto grosso**.

Concerto grosso. A type of concerto, most common in the late Baroque period, in which three (or occasionally more) soloists, known as the concertino, are contrasted with the sound of a larger group of string instruments, known as the ripieno.

Conjunct. Melodic movement by step rather than leap. Opposite of **disjunct**.

Continuo. Short for 'basso continuo' (Italian for 'continuous bass'), and used chiefly in Baroque music. Refers to an instrumental bass line (most commonly played by cello(s)), together with an improvised accompaniment on keyboard or lute, which supplies full harmony that might otherwise be lacking.

Contrapuntal. Adjective to describe music that uses **counterpoint**.

Coro. A Spanish word for choir or chorus.

Countermelody. An independent melody that complements a more prominent theme.

Counterpoint. Two or more melodic lines (usually rhythmically contrasted), each significant in itself, which are played or sung together at the same time – in contrast to **homophony**, in which one part has the melody and the other parts accompany. The term 'polyphonic' is often used as a synonym for contrapuntal.

Cross rhythm. The use of two or more very different rhythms simultaneously in different parts. One rhythm may imply one metre (or time signature), while another implies a different one.

Development. The central part of a **sonata-form** movement, placed between the exposition and the recapitulation, and containing the development of ideas already heard in the exposition.

Dialogue. When two or more instruments or voices have a musical 'conversation', with the individual parts responding to one another.

Diatonic. A diatonic note is one that belongs to the scale of the key currently in use. For example, in D major the notes D, E and F♯ are diatonic. A diatonic passage of music just uses notes that belong to the current key.

Diminished interval. An interval that is one semitone narrower than a minor or perfect interval. For example, a diminished 4th (G♯–C) is one semitone narrower than a perfect 4th (G–C).

Diminished 7th chord. A dissonant four-note chord made up of superimposed minor 3rds (for example C♯–E–G–B♭).

Disjunct. Melodic movement by leap rather than step. Opposite of **conjunct**.

Dissonance. Any note not a major or minor 3rd or 6th, perfect 5th, unison or perfect octave above the lowest-sounding part is strictly a dissonance. Triads in root position or in first inversion are therefore the only chords that have no dissonance. Some dissonances, particularly **suspensions** and **appoggiaturas**, add harmonic tension and can help make the music more expressive; others, notably **passing** and auxiliary notes, provide rhythmic and melodic decoration.

Dominant 7th. A dissonant four-note chord built on the dominant note of the scale. It includes the dominant triad plus a minor 7th above the root.

Double-stopping. The playing of two notes simultaneously on adjacent strings of a string instrument.

Drone. A sustained note (or sometimes sustained tonic and dominant notes) against which other parts play or sing melodies, especially in music that shows some folk influence. There is not necessarily any dissonance as there is with a **pedal**.

Episode. A passage of music between two statements of the same (or similar) musical material.

Exposition. The first section of a **sonata-form** movement, typically including the first subject in the tonic and the second subject in a related key.

False relation. The occurrence of the ordinary and chromatically altered versions of the same note (such as F♮ and F♯) in two different parts at the same time, or in close proximity.

Falsetto. A vocal technique used by men to sing notes higher than those within their normal voice range.

Fill. A short passage of music between two sections of a melody.

Fortepiano. A term used to refer to an early type of piano from the 18th century, with a wooden rather than metal frame.

Fortspinnung. The spinning out and development of a melody line through techniques such as repetition, sequence, inversion and so on. The term is most frequently applied in analysis of Baroque music.

Fugato. A passage in a fugal style that forms part of a larger piece of music.

Functional harmony. A type of harmony that has the *function* of defining a major or minor key, in particular through chords on the tonic and dominant, with a special emphasis on **perfect cadences**.

Galliard. A fast triple-time dance of the **Renaissance** era, usually consisting of three repeated sections (AA, BB, CC).

German 6th chord. A type of augmented chord containing the root and notes a major 3rd, perfect 5th and augmented 6th above it.

Glissando. A slide from one pitch to another.

Grace note. A short ornamental note printed in small type. The most common grace note is the acciaccatura.

Half-diminished chord. A dissonant four-note chord made up of the root and a minor 3rd, diminished 5th and minor 7th above it.

Harmonic rhythm. The rate at which the harmony changes in a piece.

Harmonics. A technique of lightly touching the string (e.g. on a violin) to produce a high, flute-like sound.

Hemiola. The articulation of two units of triple time (strong–weak–weak, strong–weak–weak) as three units of duple time (strong–weak, strong–weak, strong–weak).

Heterophony. A texture in which a melody is performed simultaneously with one or more rhythmically and/or melodically varied versions of itself.

Hocket. From the medieval French for 'hiccup', this is a compositional technique in which two or more voices or instruments sing or play in alternation. In the original medieval practice of hocket, a single melody is distributed between two or more voices such that one sounds while the other(s) rest(s), and so on in alternation.

Homophony. A texture in which one part has a melody and the other parts accompany, in contrast to contrapuntal writing, where each part has independent melodic and rhythmic interest.

Homorhythmic. *See* **Chordal**.

Idiomatic. Describes music that exploits the capabilities of a particular instrument (or instruments), and that is unsuited to other instruments as a result.

Imitation. When a melodic idea in one part is immediately repeated in another part (exactly or inexactly), at the same or a different pitch, while the first part continues. The adjective is 'imitative'.

Imperfect cadence. An open-ended or inconclusive cadence ending with the dominant chord (V). The preceding chord is usually I, ii or IV.

Improvisation. The spontaneous creation of new music during a performance, often based on existing material (such as a chord pattern). Characteristic of jazz music in particular.

Inversion. When a chord has a note other than the root in the lowest part, it is an inversion. In a first-inversion chord the 3rd of the chord is the lowest part, and in a second-inversion chord the 5th. For example, a triad of F major in first inversion is A–C–F, and in second inversion is C–F–A.

Lied. German for song, but used in English to refer specifically to 19th-century settings of German poetry for an accompanied solo voice.

Madrigal. Usually a secular (non-church) song, often about love in a country setting. Most are for unaccompanied voices.

Melisma. In vocal music, a group of notes sung to a single syllable, often for expressive purposes or **word-painting**. The adjective is 'melismatic'.

Melody-dominated homophony. As with 'ordinary' homophony, a texture in which one part has a melody and the other parts accompany. With melody-dominated homophony, however, the melody stands apart from the accompaniment particularly clearly and strongly.

Metre. Concerns the identity, grouping and subdivision of beats, as indicated by a time signature. E.g. the time signature $\frac{3}{4}$ indicates a simple triple metre, in which each bar consists of three crotchet beats.

Middle eight. In pop music, a contrasting section, often lasting eight bars, that prepares for the return of the main section.

Minuet and trio. A minuet is a dance in simple triple metre of French origin. 17th- and 18th-century composers often included pieces entitled 'Minuet' in suites and symphonies, but for listening to, not for dancing. A minuet was generally played through twice, with a 'trio' in between (another minuet in all but name).

Mixolydian mode. A scale that uses the following pattern of tones (T) and semitones (s): T–T–s–T–T–s–T. When starting on G, it consists of all the white notes within one octave on a keyboard.

Modal. A term often used to refer to music based on a **mode** rather than on major or minor keys.

Mode. A type of seven-note scale. Usually the term refers to scales other than the diatonic major and minor ones, such as the **Aeolian mode** and the **Mixolydian mode**.

Modulation. A change of key, or the process of changing key.

Monophony. Music consisting only of a single melodic line.

Monotone. A single sustained note or a succession of notes on the same pitch.

Motif. A short but distinctive musical idea that is developed in various ways in order to create a longer passage of music.

Multiple-stopping. The playing of two or more notes simultaneously on adjacent strings of a string instrument.

Neapolitan 6th chord. A chromatic chord (often in a minor key) consisting of the first inversion of the major chord formed on the flattened supertonic. For example, in D minor the Neapolitan 6th consists of the notes G–B♭–E♭.

Neoclassical. A term used for music in which the composer revives elements from an earlier style (not necessarily a Classical one). These elements normally exist alongside more up-to-date ones.

Ornamentation. The addition of melodic decoration, often through the use of ornaments such as trills and grace notes.

Ostinato. A repeating melodic, harmonic or rhythmic **motif**, heard continuously throughout part or the whole of a piece.

Outro. A section that finishes off a piece of music. Similar to the term coda but generally applied to pop rather than classical music.

Parallelism. Movement of two parts in the same direction, with the interval between them remaining essentially the same. Parallel 3rds (usually with a mixture of major and minor 3rds) are common in many styles; parallel perfect 5ths are avoided in some. The opposite of contrary motion.

Passing note. A non-chord note approached and quitted by a step in the same direction, often filling in a melodic gap of a 3rd (e.g. A between G and B, where G and B are harmony notes).

Pavane. Slow, quadruple-time dance of the **Renaissance** era, usually consisting of three repeated sections (AABBCC).

Pedal. A sustained or repeated note, usually in a low register, over which changing harmonies occur. A pedal on the fifth note of the scale (a dominant pedal) tends to create a sense of expectation in advance of a perfect cadence; a pedal on the key note (a tonic pedal) can create a feeling of repose.

Pentatonic. A scale made up of five notes, most frequently the first, second, third, fifth and sixth degrees of a major scale (for example, the major pentatonic scale of C is C–D–E–G–A).

Perfect cadence. A cadence ending with the tonic chord (I), preceded by the dominant (V or V⁷) – appropriate where some degree of finality is required.

Periodic phrasing. Where phrases of regular length are balanced in pairs. The terms 'antecedent' and 'consequent' are sometimes applied to each phrase in the pair.

Phrygian cadence. A type of **imperfect** cadence, in which the dominant chord (V) is preceded by the first inversion of the subdominant (IVb). It is used chiefly in minor keys, and particularly in **Baroque** music.

Piano quintet. A chamber-music ensemble of five players (piano and four string instruments).

Pizzicato. A direction to pluck, instead of bow, string(s) on a violin, viola, cello or double bass.

Plagal cadence. A cadence ending with the tonic chord (I), preceded by the subdominant (IV).

Plainchant. Monophonic vocal music of the early Christian church.

Plainsong. *See* **Plainchant**.

Polyphonic. This term has a similar meaning to **contrapuntal**, but tends to be used for vocal not instrumental music.

Quartal harmony. Harmony based on the interval of a 4th (e.g. with chords such as A–D–G), rather than on the interval of a 3rd (as in triads and 7th chords).

Recapitulation. In a **sonata-form** movement, the section that follows the development. It is often closely based on the exposition, but normally both starts and ends in the tonic key.

Reggae. A genre of popular music originating in Jamaica, with roots in ska and **rocksteady**. It has a distinctive rhythmic style characterised by off-beat accents.

Relative major and minor. Keys that have the same key signature but a different scale (e.g. F major and D minor, both with a key signature of one flat). A relative minor is three semitones lower than its relative major.

Renaissance. Refers to music written between about 1400 and 1600.

Retrograde. The pitches of a previously heard melody or rhythm presented in reverse order.

Rhythm and blues. A harder-edged form of blues that emerged in American cities in the 1940s.

Riff. A short, catchy melodic figure, repeated like an **ostinato** and commonly found in rock, pop and jazz.

Ripieno. The main ensemble in a **concerto grosso** (as opposed to the small group of soloists known as the **concertino**).

Ritornello form. A structure used in Baroque music in which an opening instrumental section (called the ritornello) introduces the main musical ideas. This returns, often in a shortened version and in related keys, between passages (episodes) for one or more soloists. The complete ritornello (or a substantial part of it) returns in the tonic key at the end.

Rocksteady. An early form of **reggae**, emerging in the late 1960s.

Rondo. A piece in which an opening section in the tonic key is heard several times, with different material (usually in different keys) between these repetitions. The simplest rondo shape is ABACA, but this can be extended.

Root-position chord. A chord which has the root in the lowest-sounding part.

Sarabande. In its most common form during the Baroque period, a slow dance in $\frac{3}{4}$, often with an emphasis on the second beat of the bar.

Scherzo and trio. The scherzo is a fast movement that replaced the more stately minuet as the typical third movement of symphonies, sonatas and other works during the Classical era. Like the minuet, it was usually coupled with a trio to create a ternary form (scherzo–trio–scherzo).

Seconda practica. A term applied to music of the early Baroque era, to distinguish it from that of the preceding Renaissance style.

Secondary 7th. A 7th chord built on a degree of the scale other than the dominant.

Secondary dominant. A passing or temporary dominant hinting at a different key. For example, in C major, an E major chord acting as dominant to a tonic of A minor.

Sequence. Immediate repetition of a melodic or harmonic idea at a different pitch.

Simple time. A metre in which the main beat is subdivided into two equal portions, as opposed to the three equal portions in **compound time**.

Sonata. An instrumental work, commonly in three of four movements. From the late Baroque period onwards, sonatas have usually been written for solo keyboard or for single melody instrument and keyboard.

Sonata form. Typical first-movement form of the Classical and Romantic periods. In three sections – **exposition**, **development** and **recapitulation** – often based on two groups of melodic material in two contrasting keys (first subject and second subject).

Stop time. In jazz and blues, a rhythmic accompaniment pattern that interrupts, or 'stops', the regular beat by introducing silent beats.

Stretto. The overlapping of imitative entries more closely than had previously occurred, used especially in connection with fugal writing.

String quartet. A small chamber group consisting of violin, violin, viola and cello.

Strophic. A strophic song is one in which each verse has the same (or very similar) music.

Suspension. A suspension occurs at a change of chord, when one part hangs on to (or repeats) a note from the old chord, creating a dissonance, after which the delayed part resolves by step (usually down) to a note of the new chord.

Sustaining pedal. The right pedal on a piano that, when held down, sustains note(s) even after the fingers have been lifted from the keys.

Syllabic. The setting of one note to one syllable.

Symphony. A work for orchestra with several (usually three or four) movements in different tempi.

Syncopation. The shifting of stress from a strong to a weak beat. For example, in a $\frac{4}{4}$ bar with the rhythm ♩ ♩ ♩. The minim (a relatively long note beginning on a weak beat) is syncopated.

Ternary form. A musical structure of three sections in which the outer sections are similar and the central one is contrasting (ABA).

Tessitura. A specific part of a singer's or instrument's range. For example, a 'high tessitura' indicates a high part of the range.

Texture. The relationship between the various simultaneous lines in a passage of music, dependent on such features as the number and function of the parts and the spacing between them.

Through-composed. A song that uses mainly different music for each verse of the text.

Tierce de Picardie. A major 3rd in the final tonic chord of a passage in a minor key.

Timbre. The element of music concerned with the actual sound quality, or tone colour, or the music.

Tonality. The system of major and minor keys in which one note (the tonic, or key note) has particular importance, and in which various keys are related. For exam purposes, questions on tonality might also include identifying music that is **modal** or that is based on non-Western scales. Western music that uses neither keys nor modes is described as **atonal**.

Trill. An ornament in which two adjacent notes rapidly and repeatedly alternate (the note bearing the trill sign and the one above it). The symbol for a trill is **tr**.

Triple-stopping. The playing of three notes simultaneously (or as near simultaneously as possible) on adjacent strings of a string instrument.

Triplet. A group of three equal notes played in the time normally taken by two notes of the same type. For example, a triplet of quavers is played in the time taken by two normal quavers.

Tritone. An interval that is equivalent to three tones (an augmented 4th or diminished 5th).

Turn. A four-note ornament that 'turns' around the main note. It starts on the note above, drops to the main note, drops to the note below and then returns to the main note. Indicated by the symbol ∞.

Turnaround. In jazz and pop music, a short link leading to the next section.

Twelve-bar blues. A standard chord sequence used in the blues and other popular music, which is based on the tonic (I), subdominant (IV) and dominant (V) chords of a key. Its most common form is I–I–I–I, IV–IV–I–I, V–IV–I–I.

Unison. Simultaneous performance of the same note or melody by two or more players or singers.

Virtuoso. A highly-skilled singer or instrumentalist, capable of performing technically-difficult music.

Walking bass. A bass part that persistently uses the same note length.

Whole-tone scale. A scale in which the interval between every successive note is a whole tone.

Word-painting. A technique of setting text in which the sound or movement implied by a word or phrase is imitated by the music (e.g. a falling phrase for 'dying').